ce
and
the
Heart
of
God

Justice
and
the
Heart
of
God

EMMA KENNEDY

Ten studies
for small groups
with Christian Aid

MONARCH
BOOKS
Oxford, UK, & Grand Rapids, Michigan, USA

First published in the UK in 2008 by Monarch Books
(a publishing imprint of Lion Hudson plc),
Wilkinson House, Jordan Hill Road, Oxford OX2 8DR.
Tel: +44 (0)1865 302750 Fax: +44 (0)1865 302757
Email: monarch@lionhudson.com
www.lionhudson.com

ISBN: 978-1-85424-856-5

Distributed by:
Marston Book Services Ltd, PO Box 269, Abingdon, Oxon OX14 4YN

Unless otherwise indicated, all Scripture quotations are taken from the Holy Bible, New Living Translation, copyright 1996, 2004. Used by permission of Tyndale House Publishers, Inc., Wheaton, Illinois 60189. All rights reserved.

Every effort has been made to trace the copyright holders of material quoted in this book. If any item has been incorrectly attributed, please inform the publisher for correction in subsequent printings.

This book has been printed on paper and board independently certified as having come from sustainable forests.

British Library Cataloguing Data
A catalogue record for this book is available from the British Library.

Printed and bound in Wales by Creative Print & Design.

Contents

Introduction

There are 1.3 billion people living in extreme poverty around the world; 800 million people go to bed hungry every single day. And 12 million children will die this year before their fifth birthday. At the start of a century of unprecedented wealth, we are rejecting a world where such suffering exists amid such plenty.

It needn't be like this. *Justice and the Heart of God* is a resource to help small groups explore how God calls us to live in an unjust world. Our hope is that through this material, you will discover more of God's heart for justice and engage in prayer and action to help build his kingdom. Poverty is being eroded partly because people have fought together for justice: rich and poor, North and South, people of all races and faiths. They didn't give into despair. They hoped and prayed and acted.

Christian Aid was created in 1945 as a response by the churches in the UK and Ireland to respond to the aftermath of the Second World War. Over sixty years on, we work with church partners, as well as with those of other faiths and secular groups who share our passionate determination to end poverty. Inspired by gospel hope, we dare to look towards a better world, where everyone lives a full life, free from poverty. And we have the power to turn that hope into action. Hope is about doing, not dreaming. It makes things change. Since 1950, life expectancy in some developing countries has risen by twenty years; access to clean water has doubled; child death rates have halved, and food production has grown 20 per cent faster than population. Yet, for many countries in sub-Saharan Africa things are actually getting worse – due to civil wars, drought and HIV.

The essential purpose of Christian Aid is to expose the scandal of poverty, to help in practical ways to root it out from the world, and to challenge and change the systems which favour the rich and powerful over the poor and marginalized.

We work in more than fifty countries, wherever the need is greatest. All our work overseas is carried out through 'partners' – local organizations that understand local needs. This is not a matter of convenience, but of principle. However well intentioned, the North has no right to impose its solutions on the South. So we support projects which give men, women and children the power to control the structures and processes in their lives which keep them poor. These projects might include providing shelters for the victims of domestic abuse in Iraq, helping people earn a better living from farming their land in Bangladesh, getting emergency relief to Afghan villages, or assisting families who have to sell their daughters in marriage to help their families survive drought.

Ending poverty is about challenging its causes as well as responding to its symptoms. We are proud to be an organization that speaks as an advocate for the poor. We support our partners when they take a stand, and are not afraid to tell governments, companies and institutions what action needs to be taken to tackle poverty.

Christian Aid is committed to building a movement for justice; inspiring people to take a stand against the gross inequalities in our world. We pray that this resource will offer you the chance to reflect on the challenges facing our brothers and sisters in poor communities across the world, and the inspiration to call on God to help us change the structures that keep them poor. Please join us on a journey of faith, hope, courage and honesty to make a new earth a reality, where all people can enjoy life before death.

Daleep Mukarji
Director, Christian Aid

Session 1
Justice and Righteousness

The words 'justice' and 'righteous' or 'righteousness' appear in the same verse, or adjacent to each other, approximately sixty-seven times and appear fifty-two times as word-pairs in the Old Testament. They are two sides of the same coin and they are core characteristics of the God we call Father. They stand as attributes for the way he intended creation – us – to live.

Indeed, when Israel was established by God as a holy nation, it was to be characterized by justice and righteousness (see Deuteronomy 26), and the impact of this was to be felt at all levels of society and in all aspects of life. When prophets such as Isaiah or Hosea saw that deep-seated corruption, rampant injustice, limitless greed and false worship were woven tightly into the fabric of Israelite society, they unapologetically raged against their communities.

If we, too, are to live as a community of believers who don't just offer God words of worship, but rather live obediently, we must actively seek to *live* more justly and more righteously, and *do* more justice and more righteousness. So let's spend some time considering what justice and righteousness are, and explore how we might respond.

◑ In preparation...

If you are the house-group leader/session leader, it will help you greatly if you can make time to prepare before you hold the session. If possible, prepare the room and make it comfortable and welcoming. If you sing as a group, make sure those leading are ready with suitable instruments, songs, sheet music and words. If you already know the words and sing a capella, you have much less to worry about!

Although all of this is good and sensible, the most important thing to prepare is you and your heart – so make some time to pray. You could read Proverbs 2:1–9, to set this session's theme in some kind of context. Allow God to connect with you through it.

◗ To begin...

What's in the headlines?

Allow 20/30 minutes.
You will need:

- A selection of today's newspapers

- Some pens/markers

In pairs or small groups ask everyone to spend time reading the papers and to look out specifically for stories about justice. People might like to mark them with a pen or tear them out.

It will probably be very easy to find stories about *injustice* but for this activity we are looking for stories that report on *justice* which has been won or achieved.

Allow ten minutes or so for reading and choosing stories before asking people to share some of the reports that struck them. Allow another ten minutes for sharing and discussing, but try to make sure the group doesn't go off on too many tangents – try to keep the discussion to stories about justice and how people differ in their understanding of justice.

You could use some of the questions below to rein the group back in!

Possible discussion questions

- What kind of justice has been achieved? Is it moral, political, economic?

- Who has benefited from this?

- What are the repercussions of it?

- Who has carried out the action you consider just?

- Do you think the pursuit of justice in this instance was worth it?

• Did you have a mix of local/national and global/internation-
al stories?

Alternatively, you might like to use some of the questions above
to reflect on the following story.

Haiti, part of the Caribbean island of Hispaniola, is one of the
poorest countries in the world. A former French colony, it suffered greatly under the tyrannical regime of Papa Doc Duvalier
during the last century. It is also very vulnerable to extreme
weather events.

Until recently, farmers in Haiti have had to pour some of
their produce down the drain. Conditions attached to international loans over the last twenty years have forced Haiti to liber-
alize its economy. This means that the country, once self-suffi-
cient in food, now imports more of it than any other product.
Locally produced fresh milk was pushed out as European powdered and condensed varieties started to flood the market.

In a concerted effort to tackle the blatant unfairness that
was threatening the livelihoods of local dairy farmers,
Veterimed* opened a new chain of dairies in the Bon Repos
region of Haiti, just outside the capital, Port-au-Prince. Farmers
can sell their milk there at a fair price and it is processed into
yoghurt and cheese. There's even a radio jingle encouraging
Haitians to buy local produce and, as a result, the dairies are
proving very successful.

This has changed the life of farmer Jean Anel, who now sells
his milk to the dairy. He says, 'I don't see so much powdered
milk now. It seems that now there is a craze for Haitian milk, our
cow's milk. We don't have enough milk to satisfy the demands
for local cow's milk across the country.'

*Veterimed, a local farmers' organization, is an NGO specializing in livestock
rearing, animal health and milk production, and is supported by Christian
Aid.

❍ **Moving on...**

How do you see it?

Allow 5/10 minutes.
You will need:

- Flipchart paper/large sheets of paper (or a good memory!)
- Marker/pen

Having considered justice in our communities, country and the world, ask the group to come up with a working definition of justice and righteousness – without using a dictionary. How do the news stories about justice you read earlier compare to these definitions? You could perhaps write these on some flipchart paper/large sheets of paper or, if you've got good memories, just keep them in mind as you go through the study. You might like to refer back to your definitions to edit or adapt them.

Western thinking often sees 'justice' as something public, and 'righteousness' is placed strictly in the private sphere.

In this state of understanding, business and academic life are in one box, with family and personal life in another – there is a chasm between 'fact' and 'values' – and so we are required to perform a balancing act between the two.

In both the Old and New Testaments, a single word in Hebrew or Greek is used for both justice and righteousness and is seldom translated into another word. This seems to imply that in Hebrew and Greek thinking, 'justice' and 'righteousness' are so closely allied, so integrated, that they are almost one and the same thing.

Possible definitions:

- Justice is... right relationships between all things in the created order.
- Righteousness is... moral uprightness and integrity.

⊙ Looking at the Word...

'Hate evil and love what is good; turn your courts into true halls of justice.' (Amos 5:15)

Allow 20/30 minutes.
You will need:

- Bibles
- Possibly pens and paper

Amos 5

In some translations this chapter is called 'A Call to Repentance', in others it is 'A Lament and Call to Repentance'. In it, Amos is focusing on the Israelites' social sins, and is crying out for social justice. What infuriates Amos most is their hypocrisy, as they tick all the 'right' religious boxes while getting rich at the expense of others.

Make sure everyone can see a Bible as it makes it much easier to follow the reading. Read the chapter, perhaps sharing out reading responsibilities among the group. Ask for first impressions of the passage, or for any verses that stood out.

You may find that you don't need the discussion pointers below, but use them if you need to draw your group back to the theme/passage.

Questions on the passage

• Catalogue the Israelites' social sins – try to imagine their impact at different levels of society. What might their impact have been on families? Women? Unskilled workers? Older people? People who are unable to work?

• Why do the prophets, Amos included, use such aggressive language (for example, verses 6 and 17)? If our church leaders felt compelled to challenge us directly, how would they do it?

• Why does it matter so much to God ,and to Amos, that the Israelites 'Do what is good and run from evil' (verse14)? Why would God threaten to destroy the Israelites for these social sins?

• In the Old Testament, the phrase 'the day of the Lord' (verse18) refers to instances when God personally and openly intervened in the affairs of humans – sometimes in order to pass judgment and destroy, and sometimes to bless and liberate. The Israelites yearned for 'the day of the Lord'. They were seeking liberation (verse18), but Amos warned them to be careful what they wished for – 'the day of the Lord' would bring a divine kind of terror. Recall some instances when you yearned for God to directly intervene in your life. Did he? What were the consequences of that?

Questions for discussion

• The social sins the Israelites had been accused of persist today – in what guises? Who commits these sins?

• Think about Jean Anel in Haiti. What kind of injustice did he suffer and how was it overcome? What does this tell us about how we can 'do' justice and righteousness in our own community?

• How do we, the church, balance justice and righteousness to give an honest appraisal?

◉ To wrap up...

Justice and righteousness are such huge concepts, standards and attributes that it can seem overwhelming and impossible for us to reflect them in our daily lives.

Use this wrapping-up time for prayer, and ensure that people in your group don't go home feeling full of false guilt. People *are* allowed to go home feeling challenged though!

There may be issues that have come up as common to all in the group and it would be appropriate to pray around these. Perhaps a number of people have felt very challenged and would like ministry. Maybe some in the group are inspired and want to draw upon God for continued motivation to do justice and righteousness in a more integrated way in their lives.

◉ Prayer...

During the session you might want to offer prayers as a group. Remembering the Bible study, for example, you might like to use the different members of society that you have considered (women, unskilled workers, older people, people who are unable to work) as a focus for your prayers for the world.

Alternatively, you may wish to end the session with a more formal prayer. Some prayers you might use are suggested here.

O God, you made us in your own image and
redeemed us through Jesus, your Son. Look with
compassion on the whole human family; take away
the arrogance and hatred which infect our hearts;

break down the walls that separate us; unite us in
bonds of love; work through our struggle and confu-
sion to accomplish your purposes on earth; that, in
your good time, all nations and races may serve you
in harmony around your heavenly throne; through
Jesus Christ our Lord. Amen.

The Book of Common Prayer

You may also like to reflect on this reading from Deuteronomy:

The Lord your God commands you this day to follow these
decrees and laws; carefully observe them with all your
heart and with all your soul. You have declared this day
that the LORD is your God and that you will walk in his
ways, that you will keep his decrees, commands and
laws, and that you will obey him. And the LORD has
declared this day that you are his people, his treasured
possession as he promised, and that you are to keep all
his commands. He has declared that he will set you in
praise, fame and honour high above all the nations he has
made and that you will be a people holy to the Lord your
God, as he promised.

Deuteronomy 26:16–19

We beseech thee, Master, to be our helper and
    protector.
Save the afflicted among us; have mercy on the lowly;
raise up the fallen; appear to the needy; heal the
    ungodly;
restore the wanderers of thy people;
feed the hungry; ransom our prisoners;
raise up the sick; comfort the faint-hearted.

Clement of Rome, first century

◐ Something to do...

You might find that you want to continue thinking about the issues raised in this study, and this could lead to the feeling that you want to do something.

Perhaps, when you were thinking through the questions in 'Looking at the Word', you spent some time thinking how you bring justice and righteousness to bear in your own life. Maybe others in your group had some inspiring ideas. Could you make a commitment to beginning, or continuing to follow through, one or two of these ideas this week? Who will keep you accountable to these commitments?

You might see where you can support issues of justice in your local community. Write or email a community leader or councillor who is championing an issue of justice to encourage them, and perhaps offer your support.

Alternatively, you might write or email a community leader, councillor or your MP/MEP to campaign on an issue of injustice, whether it is local or global. Look up the following sites for current campaigns:

www.christianaid.org.uk
www.oxfam.co.uk
www.speak.org.uk

Session 2
Climate Change – the Water of Life

'You never miss the water till the
well has run dry'

(Irish proverb)

Everyone, it seems, is now talking about climate change. It's not just the concern of a few eco-warriors – it's in the media, is becoming a political issue, and more and more individuals are becoming aware of their own carbon footprint.

But it's not so often that we hear that climate change is an issue of justice. But it is, and we don't have to go further than Kenya to see why.

The people of Kenya have always been at the mercy of drought and ensuing famine. But the effects of climate change are making people even more vulnerable to their environment. There is no doubt that the country is getting warmer. In some places temperatures have increased by more than 3.5 degrees centigrade in the past twenty years. The human effects of this are devastating. The glaciers of Mount Kenya and Mount Kilimanjaro are melting, leading to serious water shortages. Land that was previously fertile is becoming increasingly difficult to farm, and the glaciers are also the source of many local rivers. Mombasa, Kenya's second city, relies on water from glaciers on Kilimanjaro. As the water supply is affected, huge numbers of poor people's livelihoods are put at risk. And when the rains do come, the ground is too dry for the water to drain away, causing flooding and more threats to homes and livelihoods.

The situation in Kenya is also leading to conflict and violence. The remote village of Sambarwawa is littered with bodies. But these aren't just the bodies of the animal carcasses following prolonged drought. Local nomadic farmers have also died, not just from starvation or thirst, but as a result of escalating violence in the area. As boreholes dry up, fighting breaks out. Conflict over access to water, grazing and land has resulted in sporadic outbreaks of violence between different tribes.

Kenya is one of the poorest countries in the world, with around 56 per cent of the population living below the poverty line. Low incomes and low levels of nutrition, health and education all limit people's abilities to adapt to major changes in their environment.

Kenya contributes less than 1 per cent to the world's total carbon emissions, but is expected to be one of the countries hardest hit by the impact of climate change. This is clearly a profound injustice. And around the world this story is being repeated over and over. Poor countries are suffering disproportionately from the effects of our actions in the rich world. Whether it's about water access, drought, flooding, vulnerability to hurricanes and other extreme weather patterns, or exposure to diseases that the rising temperatures have encouraged to grow, the story remains the same: poor people do not have the means to protect themselves against the power of the changing climate.

○ In Preparation...

As with other sessions, try to make time for a little planning – think about seating, any music you might use and the ubiquitous biscuits – and, more especially, a few moments of prayer before your house group arrive.

You might like to read 2 Peter 3:5 and focus your thoughts around ideas about rights, privilege, responsibility and justice.

○ To begin...

Aqua vita

Allow 5/10 minutes.
You will need:

- A gallon (or large) bottle of water
- Glasses or plastic cups (if drinking water)

Open up the evening by thinking about water, a basic foundation of life, but one which has the power to *take* life – or, at the very least, to make it a difficult struggle. For those of us whose only worry about our essential water supply is a hosepipe ban once every few years, it might be almost impossible to imagine how the changing climate is intensifying situations in which water erodes, rather than gives, life.

Have a gallon bottle of water, or the largest bottle you can find, and use it as a focus for this introductory part of the session. Perhaps you could set the bottle somewhere where everyone will be able to see it as you focus your thoughts around water, God and your responses.

Pour your friends a drink each from the bottle (or use it to make the hot drinks you need). As people drink their water, ask them to reflect on their day and chart when, where and for what purposes they used water.

If someone has personal experience of a water shortage, ask them to share their story. If anyone else has ever visited a country at a time when it was experiencing a water shortage, ask if they too would share their memories.

You might also check out what the group knows about the global situation regarding water. If you need a few prompts, you might refer to the introduction above or to the following snippets of information.

• Scientists believe that climate change will lead to a wetter world – but not all of this water will end up where it is need-ed. Warmer, wetter weather will see malaria, which currently kills up to 3 million people a year, spread to new territories.

• The twin threats of drought and famine are caused by increasingly unpredictable rain patterns in tropical areas.

• Melting ice caps, combined with the thermal expansion of oceans, means that sea levels are set to rise dramatically. A rise of 1 metre would displace 10 million peo-ple in Vietnam and 8 million in Egypt, as well as submerging 18 per cent of Bangladesh.

• Millions of people across the world depend on melting snow and glaciers for water. These glaciers are disappearing: once they are gone, they cannot be replaced.

◉ Moving on...

'Here there is a really bad drought. So many people are suffering...' (Naomi, Kenya)

Allow 15/20 minutes.

Use this part of the session to move on from thinking generally about water to begin considering a particular country. As before, if anyone has experience or knowledge of a country which struggles with water problems, then share this with the group. Alternatively, Kenya is featured here as a country you could focus on.

The eastern province of Kenya is prone to drought, and the effects of this are devastating, as most people rely on agriculture for livelihoods. With the recurring droughts brought about by climate change, poor farmers are stuck in an ever-tightening poverty trap, careering from crisis to crisis, periodically relying on emergency aid. People are left with very few choices when drought strikes – women and children often have the least of all. In the area, sex work has fast become the only resort for many of them: some of the children are as young as seven.

BIDII is a local NGO supported by Christian Aid. It aims to enable rural communities to find appropriate and local solutions to the problems they face, and to equip people with the necessary resources to build on these solutions. BIDII argues very strongly against any project that encourages dependency and instead bases all its projects on the principle that 'what is built together lasts longer.'

BIDII has worked with Naomi Mutisya's family for a long time. They have shown them how to dig trenches, loosening the soil to absorb any rain, giving the plants more water. They have also encouraged them to cultivate short maturing vegetables that take less time to grow – so more can be produced. The family now has a big pot to harvest rainwater, and this has helped them to water their plants. Fifteen-year-old Naomi says,

> BIDII is doing us good. We have water, we have food. Here there is a really bad drought and so many people in this country are suffering. But if you look at our maize, it has grown, even when there was no rain. We have enough food. We never used to grow vegetables, but BIDII showed us how.

BIDII trained Naomi's mother in screen printing, meaning that she earns some money from selling her cloth. The family are now able to pay for Naomi's school fees.

Possible points for discussion

- What has struck you most about what you have just heard/read?

- What are the key injustices that stand out for you?

- If you lived in Kenya, how might the changing climate impact your life?

- Explore the areas you think the water situation impacts upon – not just individuals, but also on communities and the Kenyan nation.

- Consider the idea of water as a right, and then as a luxury.

○ **Looking at the Word...**

'To all who are thirsty I will give freely from the springs
  of the water of life.' (Revelation 21:6)

Allow 15/20 minutes (or less if you have spent more time on the 'Moving on...' section).
You will need:

• Bibles

Revelation 21:1–6

This chapter is about hope, purity and eternal blessedness, which comes as a result of divine judgment (see chapter 20). It speaks about the correlation between the spiritual and physical and God's incredible generosity, even in the face of our disregard and contempt.

Make sure everyone can see a Bible as it makes it much easier to follow the reading. Read the verses, perhaps sharing out reading responsibilities among the group. Ask for first impressions of the passage, or for any verses that stood out.

You may find that you don't need the discussion pointers below, but use them if you need to draw your group back to the theme/passage.

Questions on the passage

• In ancient times, Jews were inspired to hope by their belief that God would renew the heavens and the earth after 7,000 years. How, if at all, do these verses inspire you to hope?

• Despite the spiritual nature of things described in these verses, verse 5 refers to trustworthiness and truth to fulfil the promise of transformation and renewal. In what ways is God making all things new in your life right now?

• Verse 6 speaks about the freely given gift of water, whether spiritual or physical. God's generosity is almost gratuitous and is without charge. Describe your response to this, whether emotional or intellectual. Consider your view of human rights, specifically those which allow people to meet their basic human needs, in light of this.

• There are a number of references of a physical nature packed into these few verses – for example, 'bride' and 'husband', 'pain', 'thirsty' – how do these verses speak about the tangible reality of human life, rather than the spiritual reality?

• How might this 'new earth' look in the light of what is happening to the planet as a result of climate change? How might renewal happen despite irreversible change?

Questions for discussion

• The 'holy city' is divine in origin and heavenly in character. In what ways are you co-creating with God a new earth whose stewardship is characterized by holiness?

• Consider your own experience of rights and access to resources to meet your basic human needs. Now think about the communities BIDII works with: to what extent is the fullness of life denied them by their lack of access to resources?

• Scientists have estimated that we have less than a decade to make serious cuts in global emissions to avoid climate disaster. How far are we aware of this crisis? What changes might we make to our personal lifestyles in the light of this knowledge?

● To wrap up...

Global issues are difficult to fully grasp. By their nature they are constantly shifting, meaning that related research, understanding and theories develop and change. Just as many leading scientists have differing, and challenging, views on climate change, so too may some (or all!) of your group have views which you may find difficult or controversial.

However, regardless of the potential diversity of these views, we must accept that climate change is the greatest existing threat to development work. No matter which political or scientific horse we back we must accept that the accumulative effect of our current patterns of consumption is endangering our planet and the systems which keep it, us and our neighbours, alive.

Use this wrapping-up time for prayer, bringing your responses, hopes and fears before God. As with all sessions, ensure that people in your group don't go home burdened with false guilt.

● Prayer...

We need to be a church that is aware of the broken world we live in, a world characterized by the tension inherent in the life-giving and life-taking potential of the natural world, while at the same time be a church engaged in the struggle to create a new way of living which foreshadows the coming holy city.

How you pray into this, or the issues, feelings and responses provoked by this study is up to you. However, you might like to use the prayer with response below as a start.

Response: Father God, who provides for us, hear our
    prayers.

Lord, we bring our weariness and our worries,
We bring the busyness of the day each of us has just
    had.
We have tomorrow on our minds, with all its expecta-
    tions and concerns.
As we plan, organize and prepare for the day ahead...

Response

In the midst of all that fills our days, help us find a way
    to recognize the blessings in our lives and from
    whom they come.
We remember what blessing it is to have our human
    dignity enshrined in rights.
Rights which your Son relinquished in order that we
    could live life in all its fullness.

Response

We remember too, that millions of people throughout
    the world are denied the right to live life in all its
    fullness
Because of the impact of unsustainable consumption,
    marginalized groups have to fight for their basic
    rights.

Response

Lord, help us find ways to live lives which protect and
    promote basic human rights, rather than compro-
    mise them.

Help us, Lord, co-create with you a new earth.
Father God, who provides for us, hear our prayers.
Inspire us, challenge us and be gracious to us as we
go about our lives seeking to live out your good
news.
Amen.

Emma Kennedy

Praise the Lord!
Praise the Lord from the heavens!
Praise him from the skies!
Praise him, all his angels!
Praise him, all the armies of heaven!
Praise him, sun and moon!
Praise him, all you twinkling stars!
Praise him, skies above!
Praise him, vapours high above the clouds!
Let every created thing give praise to the Lord,
for he issued his command, and they came into
being.
He set them in place forever and forever.
His decree will never be revoked.

Psalm 148:1–6

◗ Something to do...

Having thought and prayed about the environment, you may have generated plenty of your own ideas of things to do. There are some easy ways you can reduce your personal carbon footprint: think about changing your energy supplier to Ecotricity, a company investing in green energy; turn your TV and computer off instead of leaving them on standby when you've finished with them; think before you travel; recycle bottles, cans and paper through your local authority or nearest recycling bank.

You might feel that campaigning on behalf of those who are denied their basic human rights is something you want to invest time in. Amnesty International has a justifiably excellent record and a really good website. And see Christian Aid's website for actions on how to end the climate of poverty (www.christianaid.org.uk).

You may also feel that you would like to fundraise, or commit to giving a certain amount of money to a development organization that supports local communities to secure accessible and clean drinking water. Christian Aid works with communities around the world who are dealing with the effects of extreme weather caused by climate change.

Session 3
Gender

'Women make up half of the world's population, perform nearly 66% of the world's work, produce half of the world's food, receive less than 5% of its income and own less than 1% of the world's property.

United Nations Report, 1980 and World Development Indicators, 1997

You may have seen these statistics printed on T-shirts, posters and postcards. I have had such a postcard tacked up over my desk for years but often failed to take in the significance and, indeed, tragic absurdity of its meaning.

These figures are over a decade old, but no less significant for that. They may be shocking in the context of the developed world, where many women are still working through the meaning and practicalities of legal equality and changing norms, but for women in the developing world, they take on a whole new perspective. These women continue to experience the most extreme forms of prejudice, and often experience acute poverty as a direct result of their gender.

If poverty is ever to become history, gender issues need to be at the centre of every challenge made to the structures and norms that favour the rich and keep people poor.

● In preparation...

As with other sessions, try to make time for a little planning, making sure that people will feel comfortable when they arrive. However, if you don't have much time, try to have a few moments of prayer rather than plump the cushions. If you sing as a group, make sure those leading are ready with suitable instruments, songs, sheet music and words. If you already know the words and sing a capella, you have much less to worry about!

You might also like to reflect on the women who have played a positive role in your own life, and perhaps also on the statistics given in the introduction.

❍ To begin...

Sisters doing it for themselves

Allow 10/15 minutes.
You will need:

- Local newspapers
- Local business publications
- Church magazine/notices

As a way to begin thinking about gender, its meaning and impact on our own lives, start exploring who the women of influence are in your families, community, church and the public eye.

Encourage your group to think broadly and not just about women who are 'successful' in traditional ways. Consider the areas in which they hold influence and what their achievements are. Perhaps you know something of the journey they made to get to this position of influence. It might be useful to explore what barriers they had to overcome and the sacrifices they had to make to get there. It could be helpful to reflect upon what it is about their context or situation that has enabled them to achieve.

You might also like to introduce Nandu Bhai and reflect on her situation.

Nandu Bhai lives in the village of Devgarh, 150 km north-east of Udaipur, the City of Lakes, in Rajasthan, India. She is a daily wage labourer who depends on non-timber forest produce such as fruit, seeds, herbs and honey for survival.

❍ **Moving on...**

The Association of Strong Women

Allow around 15 minutes.

Here you will find out more about Nandu Bhai. It could be useful to consider her story from the position from which you approached those of other women of influence.

Perhaps have someone in your group read Nandu's words – encourage people to really see it from the perspective of the first person.

Nandu is a member of The Association of Strong Women Alone (ASWA), an organization with a membership of over seventeen thousand women.* Each woman pays eleven rupees (14p/19c) to be a life member. The membership is largely comprised of women who are widowed or single, and daily wage labourers from Adivasi (tribal people) or Dalit communities.Nandu says,

'ASWA held a meeting [in my district] with the aim of bringing women together. I attended this, and from then became involved in mobilizing women from my village. When I first began to attend these meetings, I used to hide my good clothes under my arm. Women were not expected to wear smart clothes around the village, but today I proudly wear them. I am not afraid any more. I can go where I please and I don't have to be suppressed by anyone.'

* ASWA is a part of ASTHA (meaning 'faith' in Hindi). ASTHA is supported by Christian Aid, and aims to empower the most marginalized sections of society facing economic, social and political discrimination, namely the Adivasi (tribal) people, Dalits and women.

From the general body, eleven members are chosen to be on the executive, which meets three times a year to take decisions on finance and the areas in which ASWA should work. Nandu continues,

> 'I am confident about speaking to those in authority and have presented cases at our local police station on behalf of my women colleagues. As Adivasi women, we are becoming strong and a force to contend with. We are no longer willing to be marginalized.'

The land rights of widows has been a key issue and campaigns have focused on enabling more women to gain possession of land over which they have legal rights.

Other things to consider

- Adivasis are the original inhabitants of the land and make up 12 per cent of Rajasthan's population.

- Literacy levels among the Adivasi people are very low, with female literacy at 35 per cent and male literacy at 65 per cent.

- Rajasthan suffers recurrent drought and water scarcity, prompting many Adivasi people to migrate from rural areas into towns.

- Some of the traditions of the state have resulted in the social ostracism of widows; the purdah system (the seclusion of women from public observation by concealing clothing), and the widespread practice of child marriage.

◉ Looking at the Word...

'A widow of that city came to [the judge] repeatedly, saying, "Give me justice..."' (Luke 18:3)

Allow 20/30 minutes.
You will need:

- Bible
- Possibly pens and some paper

Luke 18:1–8

This is a story about a persistent widow – a woman with tenacity and a drive to secure justice for herself and, as a consequence, impact the lives of other women. While Jesus did not go on to describe the impact on her community we can begin to explore that now, keeping Nandu Bhai's story in mind.

Make sure everyone can see a Bible as it makes it much easier to follow the reading. Read the chapter, perhaps sharing out reading responsibilities among the group. Ask for first impressions of the passage, or for any verses that stood out.

You may find that you don't need the discussion pointers below, but use them if you need to draw your group back to the theme/passage.

Questions on the passage and for discussion

- Courts in New Testament times were frequently corrupt, and bribery was often the only way to bring cases to the attention of the judge. Do you have any recent examples of unethical legal practices from your own lives? What impact do unethical practices have on an individual, a community, a nation – and, indeed, on a gender?

• The widow was at a disadvantage, mainly because of her gender. Women, especially widows or single women, were largely disenfranchised and held little political or economic sway. What might this injustice – and that experienced by women all over the world – have to say about how we understand relationships between women and men?

• What cultural factors might affect both men and women in their behaviour and so compromise gender equality?

• The widow did not give up. She came to the judge again and again, appealing for justice. Why did Jesus teach using a story about tenacity? Why does holding on matter? Is there a relationship between praying and losing heart?

• Nandu Bhai and the other members of ASWA are looking for justice, and they need to be persistent if they are to secure it. Discuss what you understand about the struggle the Adivasis face.

• How do we, as individuals and as churches, create or maintain ethical practices and relationships?

• The values the judge in this story lives and works by are in conflict with what we know to be the two greatest commandments – that is, loving God and loving our neighbour. Where do we face these conflicts in our lives?

◉ To wrap up...

Nandu Bhai and the widow in this passage are not looking for the upper hand or for an advantage. They are not looking to disempower men. They, and millions of women like them, rail against the religious, social, political and economic structures that keep them at the edge or at the bottom of society. They are asking for justice. The women who go through labour without a trained attendant, the women who are abused as punishment, the girls who are subjected to genital mutilation – they need justice. The women and girls who walk for miles every day for clean water, the girls who have to forgo their education so that brothers can go to school – they need justice. The women who have done everything to support their families and are finally forced to sell themselves – they need justice.

The passage from Luke 18 illustrates God's desire for justice and his understanding of our needs. It also reminds us that God works through human beings to ensure that justice is executed, rather than reaching down with a giant cosmic hand to make things right.

Use this wrapping-up time for prayer, bringing your responses, hopes and fears before God. As with all sessions, ensure that people in your group don't go home burdened with false guilt or worry.

◉ Prayer...

The passage used here, and perhaps our own experience, has something to say about prayer. Persistence is often a necessary part of a prayer life and demonstrates faith in God's character and timing. And it is what can get us through the troughs in our spiritual life, when we are dogged with questions such as 'When?' or 'Why now?' or 'How could you?'

When we no longer believe a prayer will be answered we stop praying, which is why we need tenacity if we are to believe that our yearning for justice, and the yearning of communities all over the world, will be realized.

How you pray into the issues raised, the feelings and responses provoked by this study, is up to you. However, you might like to use the following as a prompt.

O Lord, hear my plea for justice.
  Listen to my cry for help.
Pay attention to my prayer,
  for it comes from honest lips.

    ...

I am praying to you because I know you
  will answer, O God.
Bend down and listen as I pray.
Show me your unfailing love in wonderful
  ways.

Psalm 17:1, 6–7

Meditation: our stories

This reflective meditation needs a bit of time and some creativity. You might provide a lighted candle or two, which people can focus on rather than catch each other's eye, or allow people to close their eyes. You might want to re-read the passage before you 'walk' your group through the meditation, allowing time to contemplate.

Keeping the passage from Luke 18 in mind, ask yourself:

• What elements of this story echo anything in your own experience or that of someone you know?

• Were there any emotions, feelings or actions which you could identify with?

• In what ways does the story resonate with what you feel is going on in the world today?

• Who in the story is like you or those you remember?

As you feel the time is coming to an end, you might like to encourage people to pray freely about what God has put on their hearts through the meditation.

Grant, O God, that your holy and life-giving Spirit may so move every human heart, that barriers which divide us may crumble, suspicions disappear, and hatreds cease; that our divisions being healed, we may live in justice and peace; through Jesus Christ our Lord. Amen. (The Book of Common Prayer)

❍ Something to do...

No doubt you will have some very strong ideas about what you would like to do in response to the issues raised. If fundraising is something you want to do, here are a few figures which might be of interest.

- Widows such as Nandu Bhai get £3/€3.98 a month pension.

- A child can go to school if her family can pay the yearly fees of £3.50/€4.64.

- Her elder sibling could go to college if the yearly fees of £21/€27.86 could be found.

- The cost of running a three-day leadership course for forty Adivasi women is £470/€624.

You might also like to plan a way to acknowledge the global women's experience, celebrate their tenacity and raise awareness that 'Poverty has a woman's face'. (www.millenium.org)

Using a story such as Nandu Bhai's, you could create an exhibition of stories, thoughts and images to display at your church or meeting hall.

If you are using this study near Mother's Day, you could angle the focus of your church service around this. Or you could just do a service about gender any time of the year!

Session 4
Sticks and Stones May Break My Bones: Conflict

How many times a day do we hear or read stories of some violent horror in our own country, or in those countries and cultures far from our own? How many times a day do we filter out those same stories, hardly noticing them or tidying them away to the back of our already busy minds? But if we were to carefully tear out each newspaper story detailing these conflicts, the deaths, the life-shattering injuries and excruciating pain and distress they bring about, we might be forced to allow the profound reality of these situations to begin to sink in.

Conflicts account for millions of deaths a year. It is reported that 15-20,000 people every year are killed by unexploded landmines, left behind after peace has been agreed or the fighting has moved on. Untold millions live with consequences such as long-term injury, amputation, emotional and mental health problems, and disease. Family homes, with the security and memories they represent, have to be left behind – often in a hurry, in the middle of the night. The global movement of people across borders and within countries is huge; the total of internally displaced people is around 25 million (about twice the numbers of refugees across the world). It is estimated that around 300,000 children under eighteen are directly involved in armed conflicts and, while the majority are teenagers, many are under ten years old.

Legal systems often cannot withstand the pressure of conflict and whole systems start to crack, leaving communities and countries open to corruption. This then comes to play an integral role in a vicious cycle of poverty. Some conflicts are fought in the name of God – though God is more often than not a smokescreen for the money, diamonds, ethnic or racial tensions, land or oil that is really at stake. This has been the case for centuries.

The faithful have been interceding on behalf of oppressed peoples and wounded countries for generations. Does God hear? Do we expect him to answer? Where is he in these situations?

◗ In preparation...

As with other sessions, try to make time for a little planning – make sure the room you will be using is comfortable and that there are drinks to hand. However, it will be of more use to both you and your group if you can grab at least a few moments of prayer before everyone arrives.

You might like to use the Beatitudes, which are found in Matthew 5:3–10, and allow them to frame your meditation.

◗ To begin...

'I saw it on TV... it must be true.'

Allow 30 minutes.
You will need:

> • Some recorded footage of a TV broadcast about a current conflict, or some footage from a relevant documentary or film.

You only need a few minutes of viewing for the purposes of this activity but if you prefer, you could make film/documentary more of a focus of your evening. For example, you could tape some of that evening's news, or you could hire a film such as *Hotel Rwanda* or *In the Name of the Father*.

Some of your group may experience difficult emotions while watching scenes of violence, so be aware that a discussion could serve to heighten these, as well as creating a space for sharing views.

The footage itself might be enough to prompt discussion, but if you would like to direct the flow of conversation, you could use the following questions.

Possible discussion questions

- Describe the emotions you experienced when watching this. What is at the root of these feelings?

- What did you (or did you not) already know about this conflict?

- Have your views been impacted at all? If so, how? And if not, why do you think this is?

- Where is God – in the story, in your views and in your emotions?

You might also like to use these questions to reflect on the following story.

Sierra Leone, a country which struggled to stand under the weight of civil war for a decade, held the world's attention for much of the nineties until peace was declared in 2002 by President Ahmed Tejan. The television and newspaper reports we in the West received only scratched the surface – the brutal reality of forced amputations, torture, conscription of children, sexual assaults and female genital mutilation was too gruesome for the six o'clock news.

The foundations of this conflict lay in the political, social and economic marginalization of young people, and the mismanagement and corruption of the diamond mining industry.

Many men who felt they had no stake in society left their communities to join the rebel forces, and thousands of other young men and boys were forcibly conscripted into the Revolutionary United Front (RUF). The RUF, which originally had the makings of a popular peasant movement, began engaging in paramilitary activity against the government and its Civil Defence Force in the Eastern Province of Sierra Leone in 1991. By 1995, the violence had spread to the rest of the country as the RUF attacked the very people who were likely to support them – the rural poor.

The diamond industry has been riddled with corruption since, it seems, the year dot. The Sierra Leonean government was in no strong position to bargain effectively with the established multinational mining companies. Long leases with extensive rights were signed for great swathes of land rich in diamonds. These same areas were home to hundreds and hundreds of families on low incomes, meaning that communities, schools, cemeteries and places of historical importance have been destroyed or harmed as a result of diamond mining.

The consequences of any conflict are long-lived and far-reaching, no less for Sierra Leone. The UN estimated that the war took over 20,000 lives and given that more than 90 per cent of people involved in the conflict were young people, much of that generation, along with its potential, was lost.

Ishmael Alfred Charles, known as Charles, who was nine years old when the civil war began, recounts something of his experience of conflict.

It was really hard for people, they were suffering, there were no medical facilities. People were killed like chickens on the street. You couldn't plan ahead for future days and people lost all their savings.

It was very common for houses to be burned down. [A] group [of rebels would] have a lighter or some matches and some petrol and just burn down houses for fun.

During the war, I moved around the country with my father to avoid the fighting and then one day in Freetown we heard that the rebels were coming and we ran for our lives. I was separated from my father and never saw him again.

Charles is involved with Network Movement for Justice and Development (NMJD), a Sierra Leonean NGO, supported by Christian Aid. NMJD has its roots in a Christian students' organization which worked to empower young people to engage with politics and so put their faith into appropriate action. One of NMJD's key areas of work post-conflict is their Culture of Peace project, which was set up in conjunction with the Methodist

Church of Sierra Leone to combat violence among young people, and to teach the interpersonal skills which many lost the opportunity to develop. Trained facilitators, or peace promoters, work voluntarily with communities to develop healthy communication between individuals, young people and their elders, and men and women. They facilitate workshops on everything from conflict resolution to advocacy skills, from literacy to civic awareness and project management.

Maurice A. Koroma, a peace promoter, says that as a result of the project 'The community is changing gradually... The situation is much better that it was before. There was a lot of conflict but this has been reduced.'

◑ **Moving on...**

What's your beef?

Allow 5/10 minutes.

If your group feels comfortable with it, ask if anyone would be prepared to describe a situation of conflict or frustration in their own lives.

Perhaps you could consider the following questions.

- What impact did it have on them and others around them?

- Could they have avoided the circumstances?

- Were they able to resolve the situation?

○ Looking at the Word...

'He will not fight or shout...' (Matthew 12:19)

Allow 20 minutes.
You will need:

- Bibles
- Pens and paper

Matthew 12:15–21

This chapter of Matthew is all about confrontation and conflict. This is one of the critical events which the Pharisees interpreted as evidence that Jesus disrespected the Law and righteous tradition; nothing he said or did from here on could be right in their eyes.

Matthew references a passage from Isaiah (Isaiah 42:1–4), highlighting the relevance and fulfilment of an ancient prophecy. Isaiah had prophesied centuries before Jesus' mission that he would bring justice to all communities, both Jewish and Gentile, and that this would be through love and mercy.

Make sure everyone can see a Bible as it makes it much easier to follow the reading. Read the chapter silently or share out reading responsibilities among the group. Ask for first thoughts on the passage, or for any verses that stood out.

You may find that you don't need the discussion pointers below, but use them if you need to draw your group back to the theme/passage.

Questions on the passage

• Jesus meets the Pharisees' intolerance and prejudice with courage and quiet determination, allowing them to wrestle with the question of his identity themselves. If this is an important lesson in way of the kingdom, what does it teach us today?

• Jesus promised persecution and conflict, but how did he equip his disciples to respond? How does he equip us to respond today?

• By emphasizing that Jesus' mission was rooted in Jewish history, Matthew (in referencing Isaiah) was reminding his readers that Jesus was not a political warrior for their times, but would 'cause justice to be victorious' (verse 20). What does Jesus mean for us, in our times, in terms of global conflicts?

• If we were to move from thinking about the global to the personal, what does the above question raise about the conflicts and confrontations in our own lives?

> To the ancient Greek mind, justice, the resolution of conflict, was about giving to God, and to the individual or community, their due.

◯ To wrap up...

Since the end of the Cold War, there have been armed conflicts in around fifty different countries, with the impact spilling over borders. You may find that there are strong opinions within your group, which is fine! To paraphrase Desmond Tutu – whoever said religion and politics don't mix hasn't read the Bible.

Use this wrapping-up time for prayer, modelling the mercy and kindness Jesus lived.

If there have been any differences of opinion, ensure these are resolved graciously. Similarly, if people have shared situations of a personal nature relating to conflict, make sure these are approached with understanding and kindness.

Perhaps some of the group have become incensed or despairing at the reality of global conflict, which is why prayer is such a crucial part of the session. It allows a space to worship, and to receive from God the hope that is impossible for us to work up ourselves.

◉ Prayer...

During the session you might like to offer prayers as a group. You could decide to focus on the different members of society that come to mind when considering conflict (child soldiers, victims, armed forces, governments).

You could use the passage from the reading as a prayer. Alternatively you might want to use one of the prayers suggested here.

Abba,
You are the God of compassion. Your name is Love.
In the darkness of war and conflict, you are always
ready and always willing to come with your healing
love and mercy.
In the midst of our brokenness, hopelessness and
fragility, you are always willing us to receive your
healing love and mercy.
Be our compass, Lord; be the guide, and direct our
hearts to yearn for your peace.
Amen.

Emma Kennedy

> *O Almighty God, the Father of all humanity, turn, we pray, the hearts of all peoples and their rulers, that by the power of your Holy Spirit peace may be established among the nations on the foundation of justice, righteousness and truth; through him who was lifted up on the cross to draw all people to himself, your Son Jesus Christ our Lord.*
> *Amen.*

William Temple, 1881–1944

○ Something to do...

You might find that you want to continue thinking about the issues raised in this study and this could lead to the feeling that you want to do something.

Perhaps, if you used the discussion questions in relation to Sierra Leone, or in the section 'Looking at the Word', you were prompted to think about tangible ways to respond.

Maybe you would like to research the issue of child soldiers a bit more, or find out what is going on in that conflict you heard about a while ago but haven't thought about since. Write or email your MP to find out if the government has responded. Offer your support to the MP as they raise questions.

You might also be prompted to consider conflict in your own life and think about the understanding, kindness and hope modelled by Jesus. Is there someone in the group who you could pair with and stay accountable to?

Here are some helpful websites.
www.stoptheuseofchildsoldiers.org
www.christianaid.org.uk
www.fca.gov.uk

Session 5
Me, Myself and I

It's hard not to be cynical. It's difficult not to feel hardened. After all, we live in a fast, greed-driven world made bitter by continuous exposure to betrayal, selfishness and the grotesque. We couldn't be anything else. Could we?

Our world is one where half its population – nearly 3 billion people – live on less than two dollars a day. Where only 17 per cent of its population can afford to pay all their bills and still live in relative comfort. Where the diamonds that grace the necks and wrists of both the ordinary and the glamorous are tainted by the blood of those who die in the conflicts in the countries from which they originate. Where we buy a bottle of water for 70p – more if it is from a 'fashionable' spring – when two-thirds of the world's population have a daily income of about the same amount, and struggle to access clean water. Our world is the place where, in our quest to live more technologically efficient lives, we have developed processes which erode soil and beauty, pollute and reduce our supply of life-giving water, and exploit not only people's skills but also their humanity.

But our world is also the place where communities reach out to their neighbours to support them in trying times, where people consistently put others first and live simply. It is a world where we campaign and get angry about injustices, crying out to Yahweh for his sustaining love and mercy.

It is the same world into which Jesus was born. It is the world in which we are called to co-create, with God, earth as it is in heaven.

Let's spend some time reflecting on our relationship with God, each other – in the broadest sense – and the world.

◉ In preparation...

If you are the house group leader/session leader, it will help you greatly if you can make time to prepare before you hold the session. If you can, make sure the room is comfortable and welcoming. If you sing as a group, make sure those leading know about it and are ready. If you sing a capella, you've got a bit less to think about!

Although each of us could spend quite a bit of time planning a house group meeting, what really makes a difference is God's presence – so make some time to pray.

You could reflect on the notion of Immanuel, or God with us – see Matthew 1:23 – and allow God to connect with you through it.

◉ To begin...

Empty your pockets

Allow 10/15minutes.
You will need:

- Small slips of paper or Post-it notes
- Pens

Clear a space in the middle of the floor or table and tell people you would like them to do this activity quietly, contemplating each stage of it in silence, with prompts from you.

Ask people to reach into their pockets or bags and empty out whatever they have in there onto the floor/table.

Then ask your group to take off their watches and any jewellery they are wearing and add these to the little pile in front of them.

Now hand out the slips of paper/Post-it notes and pens and ask people to jot down their incomes or job titles and the number of rooms in their home, before folding the slip of paper and adding it to the pile.

Ask your group to leave their piles of keys, watches, jewellery and whatever else there for the rest of the session.

You might like to use the following as prompts for discussion.

• How did it feel to empty your pockets? Did you experience any unexpected feelings?

• What does your pile of items mean to you? What do they symbolize?

• Are there any items which you could, if you had to, leave behind? What are they? How would you decide?

◉ Moving on...

Tell me about...

Allow 10/15 minutes.

Ask your group to think of someone they know personally or have read about whose lifestyle and attitude towards the world and living in it seems to live out God's commitment to nurturing and developing creation, both human and non-human, rather than clog and choke it. Ask a few people to share their stories. You might like to use the following as prompts.

• Can you think of someone in your own life, the life of a friend or someone you have heard about, whose lifestyle mirrored (or mirrors) God's love for creation?

• What was/is challenging about their attitudes? What is inspiring?

- If you know, what was/is their motivation? How did/do they sustain their choices?

- What difference does their lifestyle make – to the earth, to their community and communities further afield, and to themselves?

◐ Looking at the Word...

'So you see, faith by itself isn't enough.' (James 2:17)

Allow 20/30 minutes.
You will need:

- Bibles

- Possibly pens and paper

James 2:14–20

James wrote his epistle not with the intention of telling his readers how to *become* a Christian but rather how to *act* like one, and wrote in a style which echoes the bluntness of the Old Testament prophets. His letter is one of the easiest to under-stand because it has the tone of a down-to-earth, straight-talk-ing preacher – which is precisely the reason why it is also one of the hardest to swallow.

For James, 'faith' and 'works' are integral to each other. The key for James is that faith needs movement and that engag-ing in works, or the working out of faith through actions, is that necessary dynamism.

Make sure everyone can see a Bible as it makes it much easier to follow the reading. Read the chapter, perhaps sharing out reading responsibilities among the group. Ask for first impressions of the passage, or for any verses that stood out.

You may find that you don't need the discussion pointers below, but use them if you need to draw your group back to the theme/passage.

Questions on the passage

• James was writing to a mixed audience of both wealthy and poorer people. Why might he have felt prompted to write in this way? And how do you imagine his listeners reacted to his strong words?

• Describe the link James makes between 'faith', 'works' and God.

• Verse 19 echoes Deuteronomy 6:4, which is a phrase reaffirming the belief in one God and also forms the beginning of the *Shema*, or the basic statement of faith in Judaism. He goes on to give the account of Abraham being prepared to sacrifice that which was dearest to him in order to put God first. Why do you think James believed it necessary to emphasize this point here?

• In Romans 3:28, Paul writes that we are made right with God through faith alone, yet in James 2:24, James suggests that we are made right through what we do. How do you make sense of this? Is it possible to find equilibrium between these two positions?

Questions for discussion

• What is your reaction to this passage? What feelings, images and thoughts does it prompt?

• Think about what happens during the week at church, house group, and in your own lives. What is there in these which could be described as 'faith' and then as 'works'?

• James refers to people in his audience who believed that some should prioritize faith and others, actions. What might be a few of the reasons/excuses we give for not integrating the two? What do our lifestyles suggest we prioritize?

• James's frustration is simmering just beneath the surface. It seems that the root of his anger is not with his audience ignoring the poor man, but rather in maintaining the belief that the words 'Goodbye and have a good day; stay warm and eat well' are a satisfactory response to his poverty. Do we, perhaps without realizing it, maintain an attitude of arrogance or ignorance?

• If James were to take to the pulpit/microphone in your church, how might he be received? Would he have any relevance?

• Mother Teresa is quoted as saying 'It is a poverty to decide that a child must die so that you may live as you wish'. As with James, this straight-talking is hard to hear. James argues for an integrating, or a harmony, of faith and works. This can feel like a constant struggle, as there seems to be no end to the cycle of poverty, appeals and disasters and seemingly no limit to our desire to live as we wish. How do we integrate faith and works into our lives in a way that might glorify God?

• How do we protect ourselves from becoming world-weary, despairing or from allowing false guilt to settle in?

◗ To wrap up...

In thinking hard about the issues and complexities around our lifestyles, attitudes and how they impact others in countries we may never even have heard of, we can easily be led into a cul-de-sac of false guilt, frustration (with God, ourselves or with the feeling of being challenged) and overwhelming sadness.

One way to work against this is to *confess*. The Latin root of the word is to acknowledge or to avow and doing so requires an atmosphere of honesty, understanding and love. Confession, whether silently with God or with those in our church family allows us to remember that we have a holy, insatiable need for his grace and mercy.

You might like to use the wrapping-up time to do this. Bear in mind that some may not feel comfortable with confessing verbally, or at least with a larger group, so you might like to pair off or pray together in smaller groups.

◐ Prayer...

During the session you may have thought about issues to pray about, for example our attitudes to having/owning/getting, our global relationships, or how we marry faith and works. There may also be personal circumstances among the group that you would like to focus on.

Alternatively, you may wish to end the session with a more formal prayer. Some prayers you might use are suggested here.

Eternal and merciful Father, I give You humble thanks
(increase my thankfulness I beseech You)
for all the blessings, spiritual and temporal,
which in the riches of Your mercy,
You have poured down upon me.
Amen.

John Wesley, 1703–91

O God, you know how foolish I am;
my sins cannot be hidden from you.
Don't let those who trust in you be ashamed
because of me,
O Sovereign Lord of Heaven's Armies.

Psalm 69:5–6

Christ with me, Christ before me, Christ behind me;
Christ within me, Christ beneath me, Christ above me;
Christ to right of me, Christ to left of me;
Christ in my lying, Christ in my sitting, Christ in my
rising;
Christ in the heart of all who think of me,
Christ on the tongue of all who speak to me,
Christ in the eye of all who see me,
Christ in the ear of all who hear me.
I rise today: in power's strength, invoking the Trinity,
believing the threeness, confessing the oneness,
Of Creation's Creator.
For to the Lord belongs salvation, and to Christ belongs
salvation.
May your salvation, Lord, be with us always.

Section from St Patrick's Breastplate

▶ Something to do...

You might find that you want to continue thinking about the issues raised in this study and this could lead to the feeling that you want to do something.

As much of the focus of this study is on the individual, his/her attitudes and working out of faith and works, perhaps you would like to continue in this vein and consider fostering an atmosphere of confession and challenging support.

Alternatively, you might like to move the focus to a community level and consider raising a challenge to your church as a whole. If you feel that James has something to say to your congregation, perhaps you could think about a way to bring the message to them – either through a service, a sermon or in an event.

Could you find a way to 'work out' your faith through actions as a house group or church, maybe by supporting existing local ministries or organizations which work with marginalized or vulnerable people? Check your local listings or with community leaders for such organizations.

Session 6
HIV

The 1980s saw the world begin to grapple with a 'new' illness which was rapidly impacting on the lives of hundreds and then thousands of people.

An estimated 40 million people across the world are now infected with HIV, the virus that can cause AIDS. Africa is the worst affected continent, but the virus affects the whole world. In the UK and Ireland, HIV is the fastest growing infectious disease.

HIV creates poverty. It kills millions of adults in the prime of their lives, leaving children without parents and depriving families of their breadwinners. It leaves hospitals short of nurses and schools without teachers. It costs companies trained workers and wrecks economies. And poverty creates HIV. Millions of people around the world cannot even afford food or clean water, let alone an education, so children don't learn about how to protect themselves from HIV. Women are often unable to negotiate safe sexual relationships. And HIV thrives in situations of conflict, where normal structures of society start to break down and families are torn apart.

HIV can be a manageable condition with the right medication. But the vast majority of the people who need treatment are denied it – because they cannot afford the drugs. So they get sick and struggle to hold down jobs, denying them an income and deepening their poverty.

HIV is often a highly stigmatized condition, preventing many thousands of people living with it from seeking the support and medical assistance they need and deserve. This stigma – partly because of the misguided association with 'sinful' behaviour – costs people their jobs, sees them shunned by their communities and facing rejection by their families. Indeed, the shame and rejection that being HIV can bring prevents many people from knowing their status at all. It is estimated that one third of all HIV-positive people in the UK and Ireland do not know their HIV status.

The church has sometimes lived with a view that illness, such as HIV, is a sign of God's punishment. The world Jesus was born into was one where lepers were stigmatized as 'unclean' and excluded from society. But he lived a life which showed how to express God's love in difficult situations and where to find that same love. Jesus' embrace and hospitality sharply contrasts the stigma and exclusion which characterize how many millions of people living with HIV are treated.

• Since 1981, 25 million people have died as a result of HIV-related illness.

• Around 2,000 children are infected daily, most acquiring the virus through mother to child transmission.

• The UN estimates that the number of orphans as the result of parental death from HIV-related illnesses will escalate to 25 million.

• Around 7.1 million HIV-positive people living in developing countries are in immediate need of life-saving drugs.

• There are drugs available to manage the virus which cost approximately £52/€69 per person per month. The British government has spent £4.5/€6 billion in Iraq and Afghanistan – more than enough to buy drugs for every single person with HIV in the world for an entire year.

◑ In preparation...

If you are the house group leader/session leader, it will help you greatly if you can make time to prepare before you hold the session. If you can, prepare the room and make it comfortable and welcoming. If you sing as a group, make sure those leading are ready with suitable instruments, songs, sheet music and words.

If you already know the words and sing a capella, you have much less to worry about!

Although all of this is good and sensible, the most important thing to prepare is you and your heart – so make some time to pray.

You could read Romans 12:13 to begin preparing your heart for this session. See if God connects with you through it.

○ To begin...

The stigma tree

Allow 10/15mins.
You will need:

- Large drawing of a tree (with roots but no leaves)
- Post-it notes
- pens

Distribute the Post-it notes and pens. Ask everyone in the group to write down what kinds of things people do when they discriminate against others. Stick these on the trunk.

Then ask people to think about how they feel when someone discriminates against them. Write these feelings down and stick them on the branches of the tree. Read each others' words. What would *you* do if someone made you feel like this? Write this on another Post-it note and stick this on the branches as well.

Why do you think people discriminate against others? Maybe you can think of a time when you were unfair to someone. Write down what you think drives people to discriminate and stigmatize others and stick this to the roots of the tree.

You might also like to consider the following prompts.

Christian Aid partner, Veterimed, is able to pay a decent price to farmers because they convert the milk into cheese and yoghurt and sell it throughout Haiti.
Christian Aid/Amanda Farrant

You might find that the issues raised in the studies inspire you to action.
Christian Aid/Robin Prime

Session 2 Climate Change - the Water of Life

On the road between Garissa and Wajjir in north-east Kenya. Women are walking for up to eighteen hours to find wells and boreholes that still hold water.
Christian Aid/Caroline Waterman

Naomi Mutisya's family have received a lot of support and training from BIDII. The drought in this region of Kenya has been very bad, but because of the new farming techniques and business skills that Naomi and her family have learnt, they have been able to cope with the drought and continue to support themselves.
Christian Aid/Caroline Waterman

The so-called 'swamp' on the drive between Garissa and El Wak in north-west Kenya. The land has turned to dust and there are carcasses everywhere.
Christian Aid/Caroline Waterman

Session 3 Gender

Nandu Bhai, a member of ASWA, a community-based organization formed by Christian Aid partner ASTHA in India. She feels that society makes outcasts of women who are widowed or single and that the stigma is great.
Christian Aid/Claudia Janke

Women and girls often lose out on education, and Adivasi (tribal) girls face double discrimination. The girls pictured here are taking part in a residential camp run by Christian Aid partner ASTHA, as part of its commitment to the education of girl children.
Christian Aid/Claudia Janke

Women perform 66 per cent of the world's work. Here, women in India work in the fields at harvest time for a daily wage of ten rupees (2p).
Christian Aid/Sophia Evans

Session 4 Sticks and Stones May Break My Bones: Conflict

Jusu Kanneh, clearing his land ready to plant (in Sierra Leone). Jusu was a master farmer before the war, but had to flee when rebels attacked. When he came back, there was nothing left.

Christian Aid/Simon Townsley

Breima Komokai escaped to Freetown when his wife and father were killed in the conflict in Sierra Leone. He came back to Bandajuma and now works as a teacher.

Christian Aid/Louise Orton

John Foday is a peace promoter in his community in Sierra Leone. He has received extensive training on how to change conflicts in his community into amicable solutions.
Christian Aid/Annabel Davis

Session 5 Me, Myself and I

Children play amongst a rubbish tip in Zambia. Half the world lives on less than two US dollars a day.
Christian Aid/David Rose

For James, 'faith' and 'action' are inextricably linked (see page 55). Christian Aid encourages people to give, act and pray in support of the world's poorest communities.
Christian Aid

Session 6 HIV

Many people in developing countries do not receive sufficient education to know how to protect themselves from HIV. Christian Aid supports its partners to provide comprehensive training about HIV and the stigma that surrounds it.
Christian Aid/David Rose

Mónica and her youngest daughter sit outside their house in a shanty town on the outskirts of Ica, Peru. Her husband died of an HIV-related illness and she is also HIV-positive. She says that the support group she attends, set up by Christian Aid partner IEME, takes the weight off her shoulders.

Christian Aid/Hannah Morley

Landiswa Buda from South Africa is taking anti-retroviral drugs, but they are beyond the means of the majority of people in the developing world.
Christian Aid/Guy Tillim

Session 7   Home is...?

Pelagie (left) and her daughter Antoinette (right) in their barn. Christian Aid partner EAB has been helping her resettle after twelve years of civil war.
Christian Aid/Severine Flores

Children washing clothes in Abu Shouk camp for IDPs, El Fasher, Darfur.
Christian Aid/Judith Melby

Inscription found in Ban Nai Soi, a refugee camp near Mae Hong Son, Burma.
Christian Aid/Ramani Leathard

Fusheina Kwansi, a Ghanaian woman, fetches water from a borehole that was funded by debt relief.
Christian Aid/Louise Orton

Avelino Bensig cuts grass growing along the trench beside his rice field in the Philippines. Avelino has been allotted some land of his own nearby but is unable to access it as the landowner to which it used to belong has blocked his access to the plot.
Christian Aid/Amanda Farrant

Session 9 Lending a Helping Hand

A cross marks a mass grave in the east of Sri Lanka where about 1,000 people are believed to be buried after the 2004 Asian tsunami.
Christian Aid/Tom Pilston

Fish sellers in Nagapattinam, India. Fish sellers, who are mostly women, did not receive any government compensation after the tsunami.
Christian Aid/Tim A. Hetherington

A disaster-resistant house being built in Madiha, southern Sri Lanka, by Christian Aid partner Practical Action.
Christian Aid/Tim A. Hetherington

Imported tomato paste being sold alongside local tomatoes in Accra market, Ghana.
Christian Aid/Penny Tweedie

Kwasi Mfum is a large-scale chicken farmer who supported the introduction of tariffs to protect local farmers from cheap imports.

Farmers weighing coffee beans on the scales at the Gumutindo Coffee Cooperative, Uganda. By buying fairly traded products, you can help coffee farmers all over the world.

Christian Aid/Roger Allen

• Why do you think that people sometimes stigmatize those who are living with HIV?

• What can be done to challenge this stigma?

○ **Moving on...**

I chose to live...

Allow 10 minutes.

Here is an excerpt from an interview with Mónica, who lives in Villa los Vencedores, a new shanty town about thirty minutes from the centre of Ica city, Peru. This is an area struggling with crippling poverty. It was badly hit by an earthquake in 2007 and is vulnerable to the effects of natural disaster. Share Mónica's story, perhaps asking another member of your group to read it out.

Mónica's husband died of an HIV-related illness and she is HIV-positive too. She cares for her four children by herself and is involved with IEME (Spanish Institute of Foreign Missions). IEME is an organization supported by Christian Aid, who run 'Health Houses' or *Casas de la Salud* in Ica. These support groups provide basic health care; education in health and nutrition; alternative medicines, and carry out advocacy work on health in the city of Ica and surrounding rural areas. Mónica is a member of a support group run by the Health Houses for people living with HIV.

How did you find out you were HIV-positive?

I found out I was HIV-positive in 2001... I lost weight and my bones hurt. I got so ill I went to Casualty. They tested me for lots of things and in the end the doctor said, 'Maybe you have AIDS.' So they took a blood test straight away.

How were you after you found out?

It affected me quite badly. I brought my husband in... He was also positive... He could never tell me where he got it. I cried a sea of tears for my children.

What work do you do?

I work in grapes when it's harvest time or I wash clothes. The only day I don't work is Sundays when I make sure I have time with my children. It's such a sad life. As I'm alone I have to find a way to have enough food for them... I get 60 soles (£9.60/€12.74) a week. If I'm harvesting the grapes I get about 130 soles (£20.80/€27.60) a week.

What gives you hope?

Berta (from IEME) comes to see us and sometimes we go to the Health House. They give us training and help me with medicines we need sometimes.

Do you take any anti-retrovirals?

When they became free in 2004 I started taking them in September until December but they affected me and I had to stop. I wasn't eating well and I wasn't getting better, then in July I came back and took them again. Now I look after myself.

Is there a lot of discrimination here?

My family don't accept it yet. It's not the same with Berta: she loves me just the same. I go to see my mum and she gets a plate out of the cupboard that she keeps especially for me. She thinks she's being careful, but really she's just hurting me. She won't come to my house any more. But as I have friends and we meet up, it's somehow not as bad.

> **What hopes do you have for the future?**
>
> I've got through so much, but I only think of working so that I'll be able to leave my children something... I chose to live and I'll do it for my children.
>
> **How does the support group help?**
>
> Going to the meetings with the support group is like taking the weight off my shoulders. I can offload everything that is worrying me. I laugh with my friends who understand what I am going through... It's not all sadness when we get together; it's laughter.

◐ Looking at the Word...

'Love your neighbour as yourself.' (Matthew 22:39)

'... he kept giving the bread to the disciples so they could distribute it to the people. He also divided the fish for everyone to share.' (Mark 6:41)

Allow 20/30 minutes.
You will need:

- Bibles

- Possibly pens and paper

Matthew 22:34–40; Mark 6:30–44

These passages are possibly some of the most well known and often quoted in the Bible. The verses in Matthew highlight Jesus' status as a marked man for the Pharisees, a man who consistently challenged the orthodox moral views of his day. Jesus lays out what in contemporary language might be called his 'vision and values' – how he thought the world should look and his role in shaping that.

Except that what Jesus does here is so much more than that. His vision and his mission is to bring wholeness both to individuals and to society, a radical kind of healing.

The passage in Mark, 'Jesus Feeds Five Thousand', is the most remarkable example of hospitality. Despite Jesus' expressed need to retreat and rest, he approached these 5,000 people with an inclusive, warm embrace and hosted a simple meal which continues to have profound implications for us. Every time we read of Jesus hosting or being hosted, aside from food and drink, the core elements of the hospitality are love and respect.

We live in a world where too many people live without enough food and drink. We also live in a world where too many people live without wholeness, love and respect.

Make sure everyone can see a Bible as it makes it much eas-ier to follow the readings. Read the passages, perhaps sharing out reading responsibilities among the group. Ask for first thoughts on the passage, or for any verses that stood out.

You may find that you don't need the discussion pointers below, but use them if you need to draw your group back to the theme/passage.

Questions on the passages

• The passage in Matthew is titled 'The Most Important Commandment' and is the cornerstone on which Jesus builds his life and his work. Check out the passages in Deuteronomy 6:5 and Leviticus 19:18 that Jesus was refer-ring to. Do they have any relevance for us today?

• There are many guidelines and laws in the Old Testament on how to treat those who lived on the margins, usually widows, orphans and strangers (for example Exodus 22:21–23 and 23:9–11), and hospitality is often at the heart of these. Indeed, there are accounts of hospitality throughout the Old Testament and some of the people involved are perhaps unexpected hosts. Take the account of Rahab, the sex worker who was an ancestor of Jesus', who opened her home to Joshua and his men. How might we draw links between these early guidelines and Jesus' command to love our neighbours as ourselves?

• The command Jesus gives in Matthew, the only one he issued, gives his followers the lead on what their priorities should be – where do these verses fit in our lives?

• Consider the passage from Mark. Who might have been present in the huge crowd that Jesus fed? What impact do you think his hospitality and compassion had on them? What difference might it have made to their lives?

• Jesus reached out to those around him – from the Pharisees to 5,000 hungry 'men and their families' – and allowed them into his life and to reach out to him. If we are Jesus' 'hands and feet' here on earth, what does this have to say to us?

• How can we interpret Mark 6:37 in terms of the global HIV pandemic?

Questions for discussion

• Jesus treated both those who were marginalized and those who had high status with a respect and graciousness that alarmed strangers and close friends. What immediate impact do you think his approach would have had on people's lives? What impact does his approach have on our lives?

• Does anyone in your group have direct experience of stigma and prejudice? Can they share their story?

• In what ways do stigma and prejudice exclude people living with HIV from hospitality, love and wholeness? In what ways can we, the church, show hospitality and justice to individuals and communities dealing with HIV?

• What does living in community mean to you as a group, a church and as an individual?

• Around 8,000 people die every day from HIV-related illnesses. Imagine the media coverage if that were the death toll from the war on terror. How might you speak out about HIV and raise awareness in your local communities?

• Stigma and discrimination act as barriers to the effective treatment and prevention of, and learning about, HIV. One crucial way we, the church, can work to combat this is to truly welcome everyone into our congregation. Consider how you show hospitality to people living with HIV, whether in your own community or globally.

> The Greek root of the word 'hospitality' is *philoxenia* which means 'love of strangers'.
>
> The latter part of this word is the beginning of our word 'xenophobia', which means 'fear of strangers'.

◑ To wrap up...

Use this wrapping-up time for prayer. There may be issues that have come up as common to all in the group and it would be appropriate to pray around these. Perhaps a number of people have felt very challenged and would like ministry.

There may be members of your group who are HIV-positive or know others who are. If this is the case be sensitive and gracious in your prayer support of them.

● **Prayer...**

You might want to offer your own prayers as a group, keeping in mind the diverse range of people infected with, and affected by, HIV.

Alternatively, you may wish to end the session with a more formal prayer. Some prayers you might use are suggested here.

The Lord is righteous in everything he does;
  he is filled with kindness.
The Lord is close to all who call on him,
  yes, to all who call on him in truth.
He grants the desires of those who fear him;
  he hears their cries for help and rescues them.

Psalm 145:17–19

I cannot speak,
unless You loose my tongue;
I only stammer,
and I speak uncertainly;
but if you touch my mouth,
my Lord,
then I will sing the story
of Your wonders!

Teach me to hear that story,
through each person,
to cradle a sense of wonder
in their life,
to honour the hard-earned wisdom
of their sufferings,
to waken their joy
that the King of all kings
stoops down

to wash their feet,
and looking up
into their face
says,
'I know – I understand.'

Inspired by Caedmon and taken from Celtic Daily Prayer
– Inspirational prayers and readings from the Northumbria Community,
London: Collins, 2005

● Something to do...

You might like to find out more about HIV and think a bit more deeply about your long-term responses.

An excellent organization which distributes videos, books and teaching guides around HIV is Strategies for Hope (www.stratshope.org). Look out for their video *What Can I Do?* in which Canon Gideon Byamugisha, co-founder of Anerela+ (the African Network of Religious Leaders Living with HIV and AIDS), challenges audiences to think creatively about the 'how' and 'why' of responding to the virus and those living with it. Their resources can be used by small groups and churches.

You might also think about contacting your local branch of the Terence Higgins Trust or another local organization that supports people living with HIV in your community. Perhaps you could volunteer with them or support their work in other ways.

By supporting Christian Aid, you could directly impact the work of IEME, the organization mentioned above, and the lives of people such as Mónica. Every month, IEME supports five people with 50 per cent of the cost of their medical tests (£3.20/€4.25). Alongside supporting people living with HIV through the Health Houses, the organization also works to prevent the spread of the virus.

IEME train forty young people to be HIV health promoters among their contemporaries at school. They also work with students in teacher training colleges and with teachers in schools. In this way, the students they teach can receive relevant, up-to-date sex education classes (a workshop for thirty teachers costs £48/€63.70).

IEME contribute 20 soles, or £3.20/€4.25, which is 50 per cent of the cost of necessary bi-monthly liver tests for people living with HIV who are on anti-retrovirals.

Weekly support group meetings, such as the one Mónica attends, costs 120 soles, or £19.10/€25.34, to run for twenty-five people.

For further information, check these websites.

www.avert.org
www.aidsmap.com
www.christianaid.org.uk

Session 7
Home is...?

Picture this: your community, your home and your family are threatened. The tension is palpable, the air thick with fear. Some neighbours stockpile food while others pack up and leave without saying goodbye. You hear of people leaving in haste for somewhere that promises to be more secure. You are faced with a choice: to risk staying in the home you and your family worked hard to create, in the hope that things will improve; or to risk leaving all that is familiar, clutching at the promise of security.

Those who take the risk to find a safer place often become refugees, internally displaced people (IDPs) or stateless persons. These people leave behind family, friends, homes, jobs and education and step into a future which is usually characterized by uncertainty, ill-health and poverty.

Refugees or internally displaced people share similar experiences but there is one crucial difference between the two terms. Refugees have legal status and have greater leverage when it comes to gaining protection. IDPs, however, lack legal status and, as their circumstances are often insecure, their vulnerability is increased. Despite the differences, both groups – millions of people – become truly marginalized and often forgotten, living on meagre scraps from the world's bounty.

The UNHCR (United Nations Refugee Agency) estimates that three quarters of the world's refugees are living in camps in developing countries (UNHCR, 'Refugees by numbers', 2006 and 'Measuring Protection by Numbers', 2006), such as Tanzania and Guinea. And those who are defined as IDPs, or are 'stateless', are also found in developing countries, with Colombia and Iraq taking the top spots for countries of concern for the UNHCR. These are countries which struggle to weave their way through the complex and myriad issues inhibiting their development of basic services and infrastructure, so the added challenge of supporting refugees, internally displaced and stateless people, is sometimes a challenge just too great to meet.

Sudan is the country with the highest number of internally displaced people in the world. In the western region of Darfur, more than 2 million people have been forced from their homes, making them homeless in their own country. In the first two months of 2007, some 80,000 people were forced to flee their homes in an attempt to escape the slaughter, rape and destruction by the government-backed Janjaweed militia and Sudanese government forces. These IDPs are in a desperate state, totally dependent on food aid and often too fearful to return home.

We are going to focus our thinking and our prayers around these people who it seems the world would rather forget.

● In preparation...

If you are the house group leader/session leader, it will help the session run smoothly if you can make time to prepare before you begin. If you can, prepare the room you will use and make it comfortable. If you sing as a group, make sure those leading are ready with suitable instruments, songs, sheet music and words. If you already know the words and sing a capella, you have much less to worry about!

Although all of this is helpful, the most important thing to prepare is you and your heart – so make some time to pray.

You could read Psalm 5:11–12 , to set this session's theme in some kind of context. Allow God to connect with you through it.

❂ **To begin...**

Rights and responsibilities

Allow 5/10 minutes.

On 10 December 1948, the General Assembly of the United Nations adopted the Universal Declaration of Human Rights. While not a legally binding Declaration, it can be used to apply diplomatic pressure on governments which breach its principles. Pope John Paul II described it as 'one of the highest expressions of the human conscience of our time'.

Here is a selection of five of those essential rights which have been set out to protect us.

Article 1 – All human beings are born free and equal in dignity and rights. They are endowed with reason and conscience and should act towards one another in a spirit of brotherhood.

Article 3 – Everyone has the right to life, liberty and the security of person.

Article 13 – Everyone has the right to freedom of movement and residence within the borders of each State. Everyone has the right to leave any country, including his own, and to return to his country.

Article 14 – Everyone has the right to seek and to enjoy in other countries asylum from persecution. This right may not be invoked in the case of prosecutions genuinely arising from non-political crimes or from acts contrary to the purposes and principles of the United Nations.

Article 25 – Everyone has the right to a standard of living adequate for the health and well-being of himself and of his family, including food, clothing, housing and medical care and necessary social services, and the right to security in the event of unemployment, sickness, disability, widowhood, old age or other lack of livelihood in circumstances beyond his control.

You may find that your discussion begins quite naturally, but if you need to rein your group back in or would like some pointers, here are a few prompts.

- Which of these rights, or others that you know of, stand out the most for you?

- Imagine a situation which led to the creation of one of these rights. Describe it to your group.

- Is it possible to scale these in order of significance or importance?

- If you had to sacrifice any of these rights, which would it be? How do you come to that decision?

◗ Moving on...

'We have not much, but what we have is enough.'

Pelagie Nizigama

Allow 10/20 minutes.

Burundi is a country which understands only too well the complex and distressing nature of circumstances that create refugees and internally displaced people, as well as the difficult journey to healing and justice.

Share the following story with your group.

Burundi's twelve-year civil war ended in 2005 with a peaceful transition to an elected government. From the beginning of the war, around 400,000 Burundians, mostly Hutu, sought refuge in neighbouring Tanzania, where the UNHCR set up camps in response. Many thousands of other Burundians, usually Tutsi, became displaced, leaving their communities as they feared for their lives.

The process of returning home has begun for many refugees and the UNHCR facilitates this by giving families a 'welcome pack' of salt, maize, oil, rice and peas. This pack usually only lasts a month – which is just not long enough to support a family whilst it is getting back on its feet, when the people have returned to find their home pillaged of all their possessions.

The Anglican Church (EAB) recognized the need for more comprehensive care and, in 1993, stepped in to provide longer term, sustainable means of support to families. In doing so, they began to bring together people from different ethnic communities. Some of the projects include house building for repatriates, livestock breeding schemes, restoring water supply systems and seed multiplication centres – issues which have recently become even more important as the changing climate affects Burundi's potential capacity for self-sufficiency.

Pelagie Nizigama is involved in some of these projects. She now has greater security for her family's future, which is especially important given that they were displaced during the war.

Like countless other women in similar circumstances, Pelagie was forced to become the head of her family when she saw her husband and thirteen-year-old son killed by a machete attack during the conflict. She says,

> When the conflict started, I lost my husband. Many people fled so I too decided to run away with my children who were still very young at the time. We walked past dead bodies, people who'd [been] left for dead, chopped [by] machetes... we took refuge in a Catholic parish and stayed there for two years.

On their return, Pelagie got involved with the projects EAB run. She says,

> I have... received two goats and a cow from EAB. When my goat gave birth to a kid, I kept the little one and gave the goat to another family. That principle is good because it brings two families together as we have a goat in common and we've kept in touch since!

As well as running goat and cow recycling schemes, EAB also provides starter packs to returning refugees and displaced people. These packs include beans, potatoes, soy and sorghum and there is agricultural training to learn how to get the best out of the crops. While the prime motivation of EAB projects is to work towards food security for returning refugees and displaced people, bridge-building between the Hutu and Tutsi communities is also a pivotal goal and this is done by giving both communities the opportunity to mix with each other throughout the projects.

◗ **Looking at the Word...**

'May the Lord, the God of Israel, under whose wings you have come to take refuge, reward you fully for what you have done.' (Ruth 2:12)

Allow 20/30 minutes.
You will need:

- Bibles
- Possibly pens and paper

Ruth 2

Ruth and Naomi's story is one of two women seeking support, seeking refuge, in the time of their deepest need; it is a record of the losses they experienced and the unexpected blessings that came into their lives.

They experience food crises, their loved ones' deaths, they become refugees and then returnees. In a beautiful resolution to the pain and privation they lived through, both women also experience friendship, love and security. While such tumultuous circumstances could create bitterness and despair, these women actually demonstrate extraordinary tenacity and grace as well as the life-changing nature of living in community.

Make sure everyone can see a Bible as it makes it much easier to follow the reading. Read the chapter, perhaps sharing out reading responsibilities among the group. Ask for first impressions of the passage, or for any verses that stood out.

You may find that you don't need the discussion pointers below, but use them if you need to draw your group back to the theme/passage.

Questions on the passage

• The first few verses give away quite a bit of information about Boaz. Verse 4 tells us how he greets his employees, and illustrates how God is in the small details of his life. What else do you glean from other verses about the kind of man he is?

• How is Ruth's character illustrated? We know she is devoted to Naomi, but how else might you describe her?

• Boaz turns his wealth and godliness to Ruth so that she might benefit from it. What difference does this make to you?

• Ruth is surprised by Boaz's kindness and respect. She doesn't seem to expect this, whereas our experience is usually that we *do* expect to be treated with respect and kindness; we even demand it. How does this humble us?

• Ruth has the right to glean (see Leviticus 23:22) and Boaz takes responsibility to protect this right. What rights do we have, or should we take responsibility to protect, for those who are 'alien' in our country? How might we go about this?

• Ruth does not *earn* either Boaz's or God's grace; rather, it is because she and Naomi acknowledge their need (for food) and take refuge in their generosity that they find it readily available. Isn't this the core message of both the Old and New Testaments – that God will have mercy on anyone who is humble before him?

• Naomi has been quite bitter towards God; we see this in chapter 1. However, through Boaz's grace and kindness, God's love breaks through the pain and grief she seems to have been nursing for a long time. We see towards the end of chapter 2 that she has a change of heart and speaks of God as a God who blesses with consistency (verse 20). How might we respond to this?

Questions for discussion

• Refugees are usually thought of as a mass of people, whereas individuals are singled out as exiles or martyrs. The author Mary McCarthy in her book *Occasional Prose* (San Diego: Harcourt, 1985), says: 'The exile appears to have made a decision, while the refugee is the very image of help-lessness'. What difference do you think this distinction makes to those who are refugees?

• The Old Testament speaks in many places of God providing refuge and safety to those who are physically or spiritually oppressed. Indeed, much of the history of Israel recorded in the Old Testament describes their experience as a people always on the move, refugees many times over. God is described as a figure of strength to hide in, a fort or a rock, but is also described in softer, gentler terms as a sanctuary or wings under which to shelter. Have you ever experienced refuge? Can you describe it? What kind of refuge does God offer us?

• What kind of experience do you think refugees and asylum seekers have, who make it to the UK? Do they experience the UK, and its citizens, as a place of security or comfort? Imagine the physical, emotional and spiritual experience.

• The Old Testament illustrates that God has a special space in his heart for non-Israelites living within Israel (see Deuteronomy 24:14–15). God outlined that they were entitled to equal protection and rights and similarly had equal responsibilities under the law. What kind of status do you think refugees and asylum seekers have in the UK?

The facts...

• The top ten refugee-producing countries in 2006 all have poor human rights records, or are places where war or conflict is ongoing (Source: UNHCR, 'Refugees by numbers', 2006).

• Three quarters of the world's refugees are living in developing countries, often in camps. Africa and Asia between them host two-thirds of the world's refugees. Europe looks after just 18 per cent (Source: UNHCR, 'Refugees by numbers', 2006).

• Refugee children under the age of eighteen cons-titute 56 per cent of all refugees in Africa. (http://www.iss.co.za/AF/current/Refugees_IDPs.html).

• Countries with a high proportion of households headed by female IDPs include Angola, Azerbaijan, Bosnia and Herzegovina (especially Srebrenica), Burundi, Colombia, Democratic Republic of Congo, Ethiopia, Georgia, Guinea, Kenya, Indonesia (Aceh), Liberia, Russian Federation, Rwanda, Somalia, Sudan, Uganda.

◐ To wrap up...

Issues around refugees or asylum seekers can sometimes be controversial and people in your group may have competing political views. While it is good to encourage healthy debate and conversation, do what you can to ensure that it remains honest *and* gracious!

Use this wrapping-up time for prayer. Perhaps some of your group have found that difficult thoughts or emotions have bubbled to the surface. It is important to acknowledge these and give them some prayerful context. Others may feel challenged, and the same is true for them.

There may be other, different, issues that your group wants and needs to pray into and you could give time to these, ensuring that those who would like ministry are free to receive it.

◐ Prayer...

During the session you might want to offer prayers as a group. For example, you could pray for those you know to be affected by the issues raised in Pelagie Nizigama's story. Or you might find inspiration for your prayers in today's newspapers.

Alternatively, you may wish to end the session with a more formal prayer. Some prayers you might use are suggested below.

I love you, O Lord, my strength.
The Lord is my rock, my fortress, and my deliverer;
my God is my rock, in whom I take refuge.
He is my shield and the horn of my
salvation, my stronghold.
I call to the Lord, who is worthy of praise,
and I am saved from my enemies.

Psalm 18:1–3, NIV

O Brother Jesus, who as a child was carried into exile,
remember all those who are deprived of their home or country,
who groan under the burden of anguish and sorrow,
enduring the burning heat of the sun,
the freezing cold of the sea,
or the humid heat of the forest,
searching for a place of refuge.
Cause these storms to cease, O Christ.
Move the hearts of those in power
that they may respect the men and women
whom you have created in your image;
that the grief of refugees may be turned to joy,
as when you led Moses and your people out of captivity.
Amen.

An African prayer for refugees, from the Peace and Justice Support Network of Mennonite Church USA. Used by permission.

A prayer for refugees

Compassionate God, make your loving presence felt to
*   refugees,*
torn from home, family and everything familiar.
Warm, especially, the hearts of the young, the old, and
*   the most vulnerable among them.*
Help them know that you accompany them as you
*   accompanied Jesus, Mary, and Joseph in their exile*
*   to Egypt.*
Lead refugees to a new home and a new hope, as you
*   led the Holy Family to*
their new home in Nazareth.
Open our hearts to receive them
as our sisters and brothers
in whose face we see your son, Jesus.
Amen.

From UNHCR newsletter *From the Foreign Land*, 2003. Used by permission.

● Something to do...

You might find that you want to continue thinking about the issues raised in this study and this could lead to the feeling that you want to do something.

If you would like to support organizations such as the Anglican Church in Burundi (EAB) and, in turn, the projects they run to help families such as Pelagie's, it might be worth keeping the following in mind:

- The goats EAB supplies to families such as Pelagie's cost around £15/€19.90

- 1 kg of potato seedlings costs 22p/29c

- A hoe costs £15/€19.90

Perhaps during the session you were struck by what you, your group, or your church could do to respond to refugees and asylum seekers in your community, or how you might support existing ministries and organizations.

Session 8
Whose Debt is it Anyway?

Mortgages, credit cards, hire purchase. Student loans, store cards, quarterly bills. Consolidate your loans, apply for more credit, extend your overdraft. Take a second job, do the weekend shift, agree to more overtime.

At times it seems as though the money in our bank accounts is barely our own, with so much of it earmarked to pay off our debts. And the lengths we feel we have to go to, to try to make what we *do* have stretch to cover our needs, can overload us with worry.

The British manage to accumulate more personal debt than their European cousins, with the total UK personal debt, including mortgages, coming in at around £1.2/€1.6 trillion in 2006, according to the Consumer Credit Counselling Service (CCCS). The number of individuals and families struggling to keep up with their credit commitments is rising and we all know a first-time buyer struggling to get on the first rung of the property ladder. And yet, despite the difficult reality of these struggles, one is unable to compare them with the hardships faced by those who experience the effects of both national and personal debt in many developing countries – almost without exception, former colonies.

Most of the income that countries such as the Philippines (formerly under Spanish and American rule), Haiti (a former French colony) or Tanzania (formerly under British Mandate) create is spent on debt repayments, which means that their economic growth is compromised. Historically, former colonies often experienced political and social instability as the political elite battled for authority, and the former ruling countries often exploited their vulnerability by making financial investments in countries desperate for fresh cash. These investments were welcomed, for it meant hospitals, schools and social programmes could be paid for. However, these loans carried, and continue to carry, extortionate rates of interest.

In real terms, for most people this kind of debt means waking up to a long walk for clean water, struggling to pay for your children's primary school fees and spending much of your time hoping you don't get sick.

● In preparation...

If you are the house group leader/session leader, it will help you greatly if you can make time to prepare before you hold the session. If you can, prepare the room and make it comfortable and welcoming. If you sing as a group, make sure those leading are ready with suitable instruments, songs, sheet music and words. If you already know the words and sing a capella, you have much less to worry about!

However, the most important thing to prepare is you and your heart – so make some time to pray.

You could read James 2:8, to set this session's theme in some kind of context. Allow God to connect with you through it.

● To begin...

Your money or your life!

To encourage your group to begin thinking about the impact debt can have on a life, consider first the benefits of being debt-free! If it would help, you could jot down the questions and/or your responses; otherwise you could just talk things through.

Allow 5/10 minutes.
You may need:

- Post-it notes
- Pens/pencils

You might consider the following.

- How might it feel not to owe any money?

- What actions would those feelings inspire?

- Would there be an impact on your relationships?

- How would you change the way you used money if you didn't owe it to anyone?

❍ **Moving on...**

'I can't send my children to school at the moment.'

Avelino Bensig

Allow 5/10 minutes.

Use this time to start thinking about the impact debt can have on someone who does not have the safety net of a welfare system, savings or a reputable banking system. You could use the questions posed above to prompt discussion.

Avelino Bensig is a rice farmer from the Philippines and, like the majority of farmers in the country, he is a tenant on land owned by wealthy absentee owners. Avelino says,

> We lack capital for farm inputs. Our products are now only getting a very low price but the cost of inputs is really high, especially fertilizer. I have to borrow money from the money lenders which carries a 25 per cent interest rate. But it's the only option we can pursue. I have many debts. That's why I can't send my children to school at the moment.

The feudal system is heavily weighted against the landless farmers. Despite agrarian land policies which aim to transfer land rights to them, most are not benefiting, as the landowners use their wealth and status to contest the transfers.

The terms of most tenancy arrangements are also biased against the farmer. The terms allow landowners to claim 50 per cent of the harvest, leaving farmers to find a way to both feed their families and try to make extra income by selling any surplus. This is despite the fact that Filipino law states that a tenant farmer is entitled to 75 per cent of their crop.

In addition to this, the Filipino government is pushing for farmers to use commercial high-yield hybrid varieties. These are expensive and need to be bought at the beginning of each planting season, because the Philippines Plant Varieties Protection Act prohibits farmers from sharing or storing seeds. This yearly expenditure, along with the fertilizer and pesticides that commercial breeds require, means the costs to farmers are very high.

Avelino is one of many farmers who receive legal and technical support from Christian Aid partner Rural Development Institute, Leyte (RDI Leyte). RDI Leyte helps farmers become less dependent on the government, landowners, moneylenders and traders through a combination of paralegal training (for example, in agricultural tenancy laws, negotiation and conflict resolution) and supporting farmers to diversify their crops and integrate organic farming techniques into their businesses, which cuts the costs of commercial fertilizers.

The Philippines used to be one of the region's best performing economies, but huge national debt now means tens of millions of people are in poverty as resources flow out of the country rather than to the poor.

Remittances, or money sent back home by Filipinos working overseas, now account for a large chunk of the national revenue.

◑ Looking at the Word...

*'... forgive us our sins, as we have forgiven those who
sin against us.' (Matthew 6:12; see also Luke 11:4)*

Allow 20/30 minutes.
You will need:

- Bibles

- Possibly pens and paper

The Lord's Prayer (Matthew 6:9–13; Luke 11:2–4)

Despite the diversity within the Christian community, the multitude of theological viewpoints and the seemingly endless combination of elements that go to make up a worship service, the Lord's Prayer seems to be one thing which has the power to generate a sense of unity and solidarity between Christians. Jesus invited his disciples and, by extension, us, his followers, to approach God confidently, to enter into the presence of a transcendent and mysterious God, calling him 'Abba'.

Nevertheless, many of us find that we often reel the Lord's Prayer off mechanically, skipping over the meaning and value. The prayer appeals to God's love, grace and mercy, so let's see if we can connect with that.

Although this is such a well-known part of the Bible, it would still be helpful if everyone could see the verses, as it may help them to reflect. And it might be useful to see if you can read it in a fresh way.

You may find that you don't need the discussion pointers below, but use them if you need to draw your group back to the theme/passage.

Questions on the passage

• Ask your group for their memories or experience of the Lord's Prayer. Has there been a particular phrase that has made an impact over the years, that has stood out for you? Do you notice anything new today?

• The first part of the prayer has Jesus responding in faith to his Father, laying the foundation for the rest of the prayer and echoing Jesus' priority to honour him with his life. When we pray this, we are renewing our relationship with God, 'reinstating' him as sovereign in our lives – a challenge facing believers throughout the Bible. In the book of Deuteronomy, for example, we read about Moses challenging the Israelites to shape their lives to reflect their covenant relationship with Yahweh. In what ways do we respond in faith to the Father? Describe how our lives are shaped to honour him. Can you think about this in terms of debt, both personal and international?

• When Jesus prayed 'your Kingdom come soon. May your will be done on earth as it is in heaven', what might have been on his heart? When we pray this, what are we praying for? God's kingdom is characterized by peace and justice and, because of what Jesus did on the cross, it is already present, although not fully revealed. In what ways do you see his kingdom present in your life? How can our society reveal this kingdom of peace and justice more? The Lord's Prayer as it appears in Luke does not include this latter phrase. Does its absence make a difference?

• During the time the Israelites were in the wilderness, God provided manna every day. Perhaps Jesus was reminding his disciples of this when he prayed 'Give us today the food we need'. Our natural inclination is to want sufficient security and to possess enough resources not to *have* basic daily needs and, while it's not correct to think Jesus wants us to be poor, he does want us to rely on him daily. Think of Avelino Bensig. What might be some of our needs that are met because we live in a country unsaddled by extreme debt?

• In terms of thinking about debt, the phrase 'and forgive us our sins' is the most relevant. Just as we have a daily need for food, so we also have a continual need to reconnect with God's healing mercy and grace. If the redeeming work of the cross is the guiding principle for how we are to treat others, how do we forgive in our own lives? How does your community forgive? If others do not seek to make right their 'sin(s) against us', how do we forgive them? What do you make of the 'forgiving' of international debt? Have a look at Deuteronomy 15:1–11 and Romans 2:21–24.

• Perhaps another way to read 'lead us not into temptation' (NIV) might be 'lead us into freedom'. How might our lives help to lead others into freedom? How might we steward the resources we have been blessed with in such a way that it reflects our journey into freedom? How do we fulfil the greatest commandments (see Mark 12:29-31), whilst at the same time demand the payment of historical debt?

• Throughout the Old Testament, we see God's sense of justice was not only bound up in feeding the marginalized but also in correcting the circumstances which would have led to their poverty. While property and power was held by a few, it was temporary, as it was periodically redistributed (Jubilee and every seven years). This would have ensured that poverty did not become institutionalized and the landless would have had the chance to build up security for themselves. What does this ancient practice have to say about the economic models we use today?

⦿ To wrap up...

The issues around debt can trigger difficult emotions, especially if we have had personal experience of it. The global situation around debt can also be controversial and complex, so it makes sense to find out more about the World Trade Organization (WTO), the International Monetary Fund (IMF) and the World Bank, which effectively run the economies of developing countries.

Some feel that lending to developing countries keeps them vulnerable, as the repayments are so vast and the conditions attached to them so unreasonable, while others contend that loans must be made in order for countries to reduce poverty and invest in development. Whatever your politics, seek God's perspective on these difficult issues.

⦿ Prayer...

During the session you may have been struck by issues you want to pray about. You may have felt prompted to do so by people in your group/community known to you, who are struggling with the consequences of debt. If so, lift them up to God.

Alternatively, you may wish to end the session with a more formal prayer. Some prayers you might use are suggested here.

Our Father in heaven,
in hostels, temporary homes,
alone on a park bench.

Hallowed be your name,
hallowed by your tenderness
for all your people.

Your Kingdom come
to those who hunger for righteousness,
to those who thirst for justice.

Your will be done on earth
as it is in heaven
by those with political power
and moral influences,
by those who stand alongside your wounded people.

Give us this day our daily bread
to share with our brothers and sisters.
Forgive us as we forgive
those who sin against us,
against our fear of risk, of loss,
of sharing our wealth,
our reluctance to follow
where Christ leads.

Lead us not into temptation,
into pride, into self-righteousness,
into denial of truth.

But deliver us from evil
that prevents us from taking
responsibility for all kinds of poverty.

For yours is the Kingdom,
the power, and the glory,
your people, your city, your land,
your glory which will transform us all,
for ever and ever. Amen

Adapted from *The Trampled Vineyard: Worship resources on housing and homelessness Ed*. Christine Allen & Barbara d'Arcy, Housing Justice 1992 (Out of Print). Used by permission.

Lord, you are Giver,
You have blessed us beyond measure,
And the desire of our hearts is to love you first, to
honour you and reflect your glory.
Encourage us in our stewardship of our bodies, our
selves, our resources and the earth.
Help us be the good news and bring to bear the
abundant generosity and freedom that your Word
promises.
In Jesus' name, Amen.

Emma Kennedy

You may also like to reflect on this reading from Malachi:

Bring the whole tithe into the storehouse, that there may be food in my house. Test me in this,' says the Lord Almighty, 'and see if I will not throw open the floodgates of heaven and pour out so much blessing that you will not have room enough for it. I will prevent pests from devouring your crops, and the vines in your fields will not cast their fruit,' says the Lord Almighty. 'Then all the nations will call you blessed, for yours will be a delightful land,' says the Lord Almighty.

Malachi 3:10–12, NIV

❍ Something to do...

There are many organizations, including Christian Aid, which campaign on debt. Find out what the current campaign is and get involved.

To begin with, you could check out
> www.jubileedebtcampaign.org.uk
> www.neweconomics.org

It has become popular for groups to organize 'unfair' games to raise awareness about the issues surrounding international debt and aid and trade. Could you and your group plan a fun and relevant event, doing the same thing? If it was also a fundraising event, bear in mind that £1.50/€2 sends a farmer on a one-day paralegal training course with RDI Leyte, which will help them negotiate more profitable tenancy agreements and therefore boost their income.

Session 9
Lending a Helping Hand

Think of the last major disaster that appeared on the six o'clock news or made the front pages of the papers. Recall the way events were reported and how you felt. When emergencies or disasters occur, those of us who are fortunate enough only to be experiencing them through a TV screen often feel unsure about how to respond in the right way. We move between sadness and empathy, relief (that it isn't us or our loved ones) and guilt (that we should do more). For many of us, a stock response involves reaching for our wallets to make a donation. It's the least we can do. Isn't it?

The immediate aftermath of the 2004 tsunami highlighted the vital good work done as a result of the millions of pounds worth of donations made. It also highlighted that in the case of emergencies, there is ample room for dubious accounting and mismanagement of funds. Alongside this, there is a special space reserved for our cynicism and doubt about emergency aid money. Undoubtedly there is a great deal that can and does go wrong and we are right to fight for greater accountability. When we hear of unreasonable or irrelevant conditions tied to the releasing or spending of funds, or that funds have been promised but, once the media glare dies down, were never delivered, or when we think about the very real risk of entrenching unequal relationships between donor and recipient countries, we are perhaps right to be circumspect.

Direct aid is most definitely not the only way to root out the causes of poverty. Developing countries earn up to around eight times more from exporting products than they receive in aid (www.dfid.gov.uk). Nevertheless, there are still good news emergency aid stories and we need to be clear that it is not patronizing to have a desire to help; indeed, there are millions of people who benefit from donations made during emergencies. When handled appropriately and sensitively, local organizations can make amazing use of money that comes from our fundraising events, sponsored runs or piggy banks.

◗ **In preparation...**

If you are the house group leader/session leader, it will help you greatly if you can make time to prepare before you hold the session. If you can, prepare the room and make it comfortable and welcoming. If you sing as a group, make sure those leading are ready with suitable instruments, songs, sheet music and words. If you already know the words and sing a capella, you have much less to worry about!

Although all of this is good and sensible, the most important thing to prepare is you and your heart – so make some time to pray.

You could read Psalm 121:1–2 , to set this session's theme in some kind of context. Allow God to connect with you through it.

◗ **To begin...**

How was it for you?

Allow 10 minutes.
You will need:

- Images, headlines and articles relating to the 2004 tsunami

- Low-key music to play in the background

The tsunami devastated many thousands of lives and perhaps some of your group were directly affected. You will know how best to support them and be sensitive to this.

See if you can find archived headlines, articles or pictures from around the time of the tsunami, to use as prompts. You could try looking online. If you don't find what you are looking for there, you could sketch images yourself, or brainstorm words and memories related to the tsunami. Perhaps you could get the group to do this too.

Lay out the pictures and headlines you've collected on the floor in the middle of the room, or on a coffee table. If you can, play some low-key music for a few minutes and allow people to browse the images, headlines and articles. When everyone has had a chance to look, encourage people to pick one image, headline or article that struck them and share their thoughts with the group.

Alternatively, you might want to discuss your thoughts and memories of the tsunami without the help of prompts. Perhaps someone in your group has a particular story they want to tell about that time.

◉ Moving on...

Living hope

Allow 5/10 minutes.

Think about how you might have begun to rebuild your life if you had been living in the regions which were hardest hit by the tsunami.

- Where would you have slept the night after your home had been destroyed? And in the weeks after that?

- What might have been your priorities in those few days directly after the disaster?

- How might you have been impacted emotionally and spiritually?

You could share with the group how Jagath and Pathmini Susantha coped in the aftermath of the disaster. They lost both their children to the tsunami and suffered from severe depression. Jagath says,

We were saved by a tree... many different organizations came to our village but I kept my distance – and almost felt like resorting to violence to release the tension within me.

Christian Aid partner Basic Needs is focusing its work around the area of southern Sri Lanka where Jagath and Pathmini live. In the aftermath of the disaster, they met immediate needs of shelter, clean water and food for internally displaced people, but have also worked to address the psychological welfare of individuals and communities. They have trained volunteers in communities, and delivered health and emotional support as part of overall rehabilitation services. Jagath goes on to say,

Basic Needs were seeking volunteers and noticed that I was not involved in anything. They approached me about giving service to my own community through their volunteer programme. As volunteers we identify problem areas and refer people to health camps.

Many of the women in our area used to be engaged in coir-making as an income-generating activity. With the tsunami they have stopped this... I took them to the clinic for treatment and therapy and thankfully several of them have overcome their traumas and returned to coir-making.

Jagath has a new sense of purpose and can now see way through his bereavement. He says,

Thanks to Basic Needs and my involvement with the community, I have been able to cope with my grief.

Basic Needs is working to find long-lasting solutions to help individuals and communities to support themselves and rebuild their lives. Isuru, aged seventeen, has also benefited from the

Basic Needs programme. He is the current leader of their Childrens' Club, catering for young people under eighteen, many of whom lost their parents, possessions and homes. Isuru lost his brother to the tsunami. He explains,

> In our club we decide and plan our activities ourselves... over the past year, many organizations have come to the assistance of our community and we have come to depend on them. We now need to stand on our own feet. We don't want sympathy but support to change the dependency mentality.
>
> I am proud to say that in our club we look beyond ourselves... the main objective is to nurture a future generation who think beyond the individual and towards a sense of community.

◗ Looking at the Word...

An anchor for our souls

Allow 20/30 minutes.
You will need:

- Bibles
- Possibly pens and paper

Hebrews 6:17–20

Hope is an unmistakable characteristic and people who cultivate it have an assurance about them that is inspiring. It is an important part of all faith traditions and forms part of the classic triad in Christianity, linking inextricably with faith and love (Colossians 1:4–5). The passage these verses come from illustrates the eternity of God's promises by remembering his special relationship with Abraham before drawing links to the fulfilment of Jesus' ministry. It is from this that we, as believers, draw hope.

Make sure everyone can see a Bible as it makes it much easier to follow the reading. Perhaps you could share out reading responsibilities among the group. Begin by asking for first impressions of the passage, or for any verses that stood out.

You may find that you don't need the discussion pointers below, but use them if you need to draw your group back to the theme/passage.

Questions on the passage

• This passage explains that because God is the supreme authority, he has bound himself to keeping the promises he made to us by taking 'an oath in his own name' (verse 13) and because he is Truth, he cannot lie. It is for these reasons that we can depend on the Holy Spirit to sustain us with hope. Is that your experience?

• Hope is a vital part of life, closely linked with good health and emotional well-being. The Bible teaches us that hope is a confident expectation; this is very different from the wishful thinking we often take it for. Just as there is much in the Bible that generates hope, there are also descriptions of hopelessness; for example, some psalms, chunks of Lamentations and accounts such as Peter's denial of Jesus. Have you ever experienced hopelessness? What other feelings or attitudes does this generate? How can we keep from slipping into a cycle of hopelessness?

• Verse 19 describes how it is hope that leads us into the presence of God. Being in the 'inner sanctuary' is also where we have our hope replenished and, consequently, our love deepened and faith strengthened. In what ways do you enter into the inner sanctuary? How do you cherish that space and time in your day?

• Aristotle described hope as a waking dream, which contrasts with our hope in God being described as 'a strong and trustworthy anchor for our souls' (verse 19). How is hope manifested in your life? How might you help to make hope more of a reality and less of a 'waking dream' for others in your life?

Questions for discussion

• Can you describe the people in your life who have stirred hope in you when your own was faltering? What was it they did to generate this in you? What difference did it make?

• Rebuilding after a disaster involves more than bricks and mortar. When the normal structures of society start to break down, normal behaviour can break down as well. What long-term implications might this have? Why do you think HIV rates of infection are particularly high in situations of conflict or emergency?

• The number of people killed by disasters in developing countries is more than ten times higher than those killed in developed countries. Also, the incidence and intensity of natural disasters is being propelled by the changing climate. Disasters such as hurricanes or floods serve to highlight any lack in infrastructure, resources and equality – and these are only set to increase. How can our society work to create 'a strong and trustworthy anchor' of hope for communities like these? How can we encourage communities to prepare for disasters? Why is it we have to wait until a disaster hits before we become aware of the vulnerability of communities such as Jagath's and Isuru's?

● To wrap up...

Issues around aid are primed for controversy. While there is a need for us to reach into our wallets in response to appeals and to commit to financially supporting disaster relief organizations, there is a great deal that can be done to reduce the vulnerability of marginalized communities to disasters and hazards. As Christians, the place to start is prayer, but it should also inspire us to action. Such a difficult issue is worth spending time thinking and praying about, There may also be broader or personal issues that it would be appropriate to pray for, so make time for this in your session.

● Prayer...

During the session you might want to offer prayers as a group. During the Bible study, for example, you may have found that difficult feelings or memories of the tsunami or different disasters were triggered. How you pray about these things is up to you but you may find some inspiration below.

Some prayers you might use are suggested here.

God is our refuge and strength,
  always ready to help in times of trouble.
So we will not fear when earthquakes come
  and the mountains crumble into the sea.
Let the oceans roar and foam.
  Let the mountains tremble as the waters surge!
... The Lord of Heaven's Armies is here
  among us;
the God of Israel is our fortress.

Psalm 46:1–3, 7

O God, who would fold both heaven and earth in a single
     peace:
Let the design of thy great love
lighten upon the waste of our wraths and sorrows:
and give peace to thy Church,
peace among nations,
peace in our dwellings,
and peace in our hearts:
through thy Son our Saviour Jesus Christ.
Amen.

From the Church of England's website www.invitationtoprayer.org.
Used by permission.

❍ Something to do...

While you are using this study, it is likely there will be an emergency or disaster situation somewhere in the world. You might feel compelled to respond so look into the circumstances and discuss with your group how best you might use your energies to bring longer term hope. Is money needed? Or could you helpfully raise awareness of the circumstances that increase that community's vulnerability to disaster and emergencies?

Perhaps you could set up a savings account to collect or fundraise money for use in times of international emergency. Make sure you set it up with the agreement of your group and/or your church leadership and that you are able to maintain accountability and transparency throughout.

Be sure to have a look at
     www.dec.org.uk
     www.dfid.gov.uk
     www.alertnet.org

Session 10
Working Your Way Up

Humans have been trading since before currency existed and famous trade routes such as the Amber Road and the Silk Route have gained a status that is almost mythological. That kind of history seems more than a world away from buzzwords such as 'globalization', 'subsidies' and 'trade barriers'. And the whole concept of trade seems entirely disconnected from the lives of people who live the good, bad and ugly reality of free trade.

In the developed world, where we can 'buy one, get one free' and sample the delights of cuisine and technology from all over the world, our experience of trade and global markets may be positive. However, the experience of many people in the world is that they work harder only to earn less year on year. Trading is a fundamental element of living in a community; it has an incredible capacity to create wealth, knowledge and stability but it has been loaded with such a strong bias towards rich countries that many people in the developed world can expect to earn less than 70p/93c a day.

The Drop the Debt and Make Poverty History campaigns along with Trade Justice Movement brought the issues of aid, debt and trade straight into our living rooms and pushed thousands of ordinary people out into the streets to march and lobby MPs. A huge amount of awareness was raised internationally, promises and commitments from governments were secured and a great groundswell of passion was generated. But there still remains a staggering inequality in the global marketplace. Our world is so tightly interconnected that even if we tried to ignore these stark inequalities it is increasingly difficult to do so. Pursuing economic and political justice is no longer an optional extra for those of us who seek to reflect God's glory to a fragmented world.

Perhaps you will be able to use this study to bolster or reignite your commitment to be a voice for the voiceless.

○ **In preparation...**

If you are the house group leader/session leader, it will help you greatly if you can make time to prepare before you hold the session. Do what you can to prepare the room and make it comfortable and welcoming for your group. If you sing as a group, make sure those leading are ready with suitable instruments, songs, sheet music or words. If you already know the words and sing a capella, you have much less to worry about!

Although all of this is good and sensible, the most important thing to prepare is you and your heart – so make some time to pray.

You could reflect on the following quotation to set this session's theme in some kind of context.

> 'A day will come when markets, open to trade, and minds, open to ideas, will become the sole battlefield.'
>
> Victor Marie Hugo, 1802–85

○ **To begin...**

Allow 10/15 minutes.

To open up this session, you could begin by checking out with your group what they know about trade issues. You may not need any prompts but if you do here are some facts, statistics and definitions you could use. If you have time to prepare before the session you might check out www.dfid.gov.uk for more information.

> World Trade Organization (WTO): the international body which deals with trading rules between countries. Its purpose is to persuade countries to liberalize or open up their markets by

abolishing import tariffs and other barriers. It presides over trade disputes between its 150 member countries.

International Monetary Fund (IMF): the organization which seeks to protect global economic stability and avoid financial crisis. It has a big hand in developing countries by setting up a loans scheme with the World Bank called the Poverty Reduction and Growth Facility.

World Bank: promotes privatization and funds infrastructure projects linked with the Millennium Development Goals. In conjunction with the IMF, the bank set up the Heavily Indebted Poor Countries Initiative (HIPC) to assess whether poorer countries could have their debts cancelled.

Three quarters of the least developed countries are dependent on one or two commodity exports for over half of their foreign exchange earnings. For most of those countries the real price of those commodities is at a 150 year low. (UNCTAD* Report, 2001)

The chasm between highly developed and less developed countries is huge. In 1998 sub-Saharan Africa earned eight times less than Switzerland. (World Bank, 2000)

*UNCTAD: United Nations Conference on Trade and Development

Tariffs are taxes on imported foreign goods and services. *Subsidies* are financial assistance from governments that can take the form of tax breaks, grants or trade barriers. *Liberalization* is the relaxing of restrictions on markets.

Many of the tariffs imposed on people in developing countries are twice as high as those faced by non-poor people, although they are often imposed by other developing countries (World Bank, 2002).

Subsidies given to farmers in rich countries were estimated at around $250 billion in 2000. That's about five times the amount given in international development assistance (World Bank, 2002).

○ **Moving on...**

'Why can't we do the same?'

Kwasi Mfum, chicken farmer, Ghana

Allow 5/10 minutes.

You can use this time to begin thinking about the human face of liberalization. If anyone in your group has experience of something similar, ask them to share it. If not, don't worry, because you can introduce Mr Kwasi Mfum to the group. He breeds chicks to sell to large poultry farms around the country and has been in business over ten years. He says,

> If the Ghanaian government were to increase the tariff on poultry coming into Ghana, the countries which import [would] simply reduce the price of the chicken, so they [would] continue to be cheaper than local chicken (even with the higher import tax).
>
> Take Nigeria, they do not allow any poultry imports. Their poultry production is growing – why can't we do the same?
>
> We are importing hatching eggs from South Africa into Ghana. Why South Africa? I have a breeding farm – if we had help we could produce enough ourselves.

Kwasi Mfum supplies Emmanuel Kwasi Gyan with chicks for his large-scale poultry business. He has been in business since the beginning of the 1980s and feels strongly about the potential impact of tariffs on his sector. He says,

> At the end of the day, people in the market buy the cheapest, whether it's local or imported. I would prefer to buy local poultry and maize but I buy what is the cheapest at that time.

I supported [the proposed] increase in tariffs on imported poultry because the local production would improve. The poultry industry is our backbone. With high interest rates in Ghana, the poultry business is very expensive. I had even prepared one of my farms for 40,000 birds in anticipation of the tariff. When the tariffs were suspended I increased the number of layers instead.

❍ Looking at the Word...

'... be holy in everything you do...' (1 Peter 1:15)

Allow 20/30 minutes.
You will need:

- Bibles
- Possibly pens and paper

1 Peter 1:15–22

When we read passages such as Isaiah 58 and Micah 6:8, we are reminded that being in relationship with Jesus is not just about seeking personal holiness but also about seeking justice. But we, the contemporary church, often don't see the pursuit of justice as part of our call to be holy as God is holy. However, right at the centre of God's holiness is where we find his passion for justice, stretched out on the cross at Calvary. God's holiness is the antithesis of the worldly, the common and is about separateness, transcendence, mystery and purity.

Here Peter challenges his first audience, and us, to integrate the beliefs and practices of holiness into our lives. Dip into these verses and work out the challenge for yourself.

Make sure everyone can see a Bible as it makes it much easier to follow the reading. Read the chapter, perhaps sharing out reading responsibilities among the group. Ask for first impressions of the passage, or for any verses that stood out.

You may find that you don't need the discussion pointers below, but use them if you need to draw your group back to the theme/passage.

Questions on the passage

• Peter introduces holiness early on in this letter and it continues throughout his writing. He describes the belief and behaviour associated with holiness – we know it is not through our own efforts, but by God's grace and that it is not easy. He describes the struggles believers should expect in 1 Peter 4. What do these verses in 1 Peter 1 have to say to you about holiness and justice?

• As God is holy, so we are called to be holy (verse 16). How might pursuing justice in our own lives be part of this calling? How is God's holiness expressed in his outworking of justice? We can sometimes restrict our understanding of holiness to worship services, 24/7 prayer meetings or church-sponsored projects. But in doing this, in disconnecting justice from holiness, we run the risk of living and teaching an understanding of these two aspects of God's character which more closely reflect our own values than his. How would you describe the values you think the global church currently teaches? How are these expressed?

• Throughout the Old Testament, we read how Israel was called to be different or set apart, not just in the way they worshipped but also in the social order they established and perpetuated. In the same way that we often do not live out the parable of the landowner who gave all his workers a living wage (Matthew 20:1–16), we also corrupt the rules laid down in Scripture, just as the Jews of ancient times did. From your perspective, what is the reality of how God's holiness and justice is currently manifested by the church?

• Believers are to be holy because God commanded it; Peter is specifically not speaking to non-believers here. Countless Christians have woven this challenge into their lives and have been at the forefront of campaigns to secure justice for others, from William Wilberforce to Martin Luther King. Who are the people in your life or in your community that challenge the social order to seek justice for the marginalized? Who inspires you to do the same? What inspiration do you glean from verse 22?

• Because of the hope we have in a new heaven and a new earth, made possible through Jesus' sacrifice on the cross (verses 18–22), we can, by God's grace, reach for holiness and reflect his glory. In what ways do you see this being made real in your life?

Questions for discussion

• The Reverend Dr Samuel Kobia, General Secretary of the World Council of Churches, had this to say at a 2007 Council for World Mission conference in Johannesburg, in response to global trade issues:

'Trade which does not eradicate poverty, enhance equality and care for the environment is not worth promoting. When trade, as it does today, sends the majority of people into grinding poverty, increasing hunger and loss of livelihoods, while a few enjoy excessive wealth, then as churches we need to intensify our advocacy work.'

What thoughts does this prompt in you?

- Ethical business practices should be the norm. Shouldn't they? If that were so, what would be the impact on your life and community? Is campaigning for trade justice a way for you to put your faith into action? Think of the policies you know the WTO, IMF, World Bank and our government promote. What values do these reflect?

- We know there are tangible consequences to justice and injustice. Are there spiritual and psychological consequences too?

- How might people like us, and Kwasi Mfum and Emmanuel Kwasi Gyan become more connected with our economies, our communities and our workplaces? What policies and practices would support, rather than oppress this?

● To wrap up...

Issues around international trade can seem complex, stuffed full of tricky jargon and hard-headed policy. The size and reach of governments and organizations such as the IMF and World Bank seem so overwhelming that it feels as if there is little we can do. Perhaps praying for a sense of possibility is a good place to start. Pray for personal commitment as well as for commitment from governments, the WTO, IMF and World Bank; pray too for commitment from multinational companies to work increasingly harder on behalf of vulnerable people, as this is vital.

There may be other issues you would like to bring before God. Perhaps you could spend time in ministry. Ensure you do what is right for your group's needs.

◉ **Prayer...**

During the session you might want to offer prayers as a group.

Alternatively, you may wish to end the session with a more formal prayer. Two prayers you might use are suggested here.

I stood up for justice and the right;
   don't leave me to the mercy of my oppressors.
Take the side of your servant, good God;
   don't let the godless take advantage of me.
I can't keep my eyes open any longer, waiting for you
   to keep your promise to set everything right.
Let your love dictate how you deal with me;
   teach me from your textbook on life.
I'm your servant – help me understand what that means,
   the inner meaning of your instructions.
It's time to act, GOD;
   they've made a shambles of your revelation!
Yea-Saying God, I love what you command,
   I love it better than gold and gemstones;
Yea-Saying God, I honour everything you tell me,
   I despise every deceitful detour.

Psalm 119:121–128

Breathe in me, O Holy Spirit, that my thoughts may all
   be holy
Act in me, O Holy Spirit, that my work too may be holy
Draw my heart, O Holy Spirit, that I love but what is holy
Strengthen me, O Holy Spirit, to defend all that is holy
Guide me then, O Holy Spirit, that I always may be holy.
Amen

Attributed to Augustine

○ **Something to do...**

A really practical way to respond to the issue of trade justice as a group is to source fairly and ethically traded products to use at events and meetings held by your church. Perhaps your group would like to take on the challenge of becoming a Fairtrade Church. To find out how to begin this process, check out the Fairtrade Foundation at www.fairtrade.org.uk

You may already buy ethically traded goods such as chocolate and coffee but perhaps you are also interested in finding out about the ethical status of other products. If so, have a look at www.gooshing.co.uk, an ethical shopping tool from *The Good Shopping Guide* which helps you to choose products and services from responsible companies.

While you can influence manufacturers and retailers with how you spend what is in your wallet, you can also wield influence by lobbying your MP and, in particular, the Secretary of State for International Development. Organizations such as Christian Aid will continue to take governments and unaccountable organizations such as the WTO to task on behalf of developing countries, but they need people like you to put belief into action.

Check out
>   www.christianaid.org.uk
>   www.cafod.org.uk
>   www.tjm.org.uk

◗ Notes